LEADING

FROM

HERE

TO

THERE

FIVE ESSENTIAL SKILLS

LEADERSHIP RESOURCES FROM BILL HYBELS

Courageous Leadership

Leadership Axioms

The Call to Lead
(with John Ortberg and Dan B. Allender)

Holy Discontent

Living and Leading from Your Holy Discontent

Just Walk Across the Room

The Volunteer Revolution

STUDY GUIDE   FIVE SESSIONS

LEADING
FROM
HERE
TO
THERE

FIVE ESSENTIAL SKILLS

BILL HYBELS

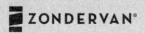 ZONDERVAN®

WILLOW CREEK
ASSOCIATION

ZONDERVAN

Leading from Here to There Study Guide

Copyright © 2016 by Willow Creek Community Church

Requests for information should be addressed to:

Zondervan, *3900 Sparks Dr. SE, Grand Rapids, Michigan 49546*

ISBN 978-0-310-08087-9

Cover design: Sue Swearingen

Interior design: Fresh Folio Design

First Printing May 2016 / Printed in the United States of America

CONTENTS

ACKNOWLEDGMENTS

As leaders know, all good things are accomplished through the hard work of a talented team. We would like to acknowledge the contributions of the following people in shaping this study guide: Kathy Buscaglia, Instructional Designer; Liz Driscoll, Content Director; September Vaudrey, Writer; Gina Young, Producer and Project Manager; Lori Hermann, Executive Producer; Steve Bell, Executive Vice President of Willow Creek Association. In addition, we would like to express our gratitude to the volunteers and staff at New Life Church and Flanders Electric in Evansville, Indiana, and Willow Creek Community Church and Casa de Luz in South Barrington, Illinois, whose input during the curriculum validation was invaluable and truly improved the content in this guide.

A Note from Bill Hybels

Dear Reader,

Judging from the fact that a study titled *Leading from Here to There* caught your eye, I already know something about you that I admire: You likely have an interest in developing the leadership gift God has entrusted to your care. You have a hunger to get better at leading—and that's my desire for you, as well! Here's why:

Leadership matters. Whether you lead a top-100 global business or a start-up with three employees; a multi-campus church or a tiny congregation that is the only beacon of light in its community; a team of creatives or a team of accountants; a project, a process, or the team of people you call family—*no matter what the sphere, your leadership makes all the difference in the future of those you lead.* And bright, godly, fired-up leaders will make the kinds of differences that will bring about a better future for our world.

Leadership development is a lifelong pursuit, and I am far from done growing as a leader. But in the forty-plus years I have been leading, I've come to recognize a handful of areas that are critical for every leader to develop, no matter where they are on their leadership journey. In the *Leading from Here to There* DVD sessions, I've done my best to unpack each of these areas in highly practical ways. The guide you hold in your hands will help you process your takeaways from each video session and apply them tomorrow in your leadership environment.

Take your leadership development seriously and go at it every day with all the passion and commitment that you can. And let's partner together to move the purposes of God ahead in this world.

Blessings,

Bill Hybels

Bill Hybels
Chair, Willow Creek Association
Senior Pastor, Willow Creek Community Church

Welcome
to *Leading From Here to There.*

This study guide is a companion resource to the *Leading from Here to There* video experience, and is designed to help you examine your leadership potential, learn alongside others on the leadership journey, and practice putting new skills into action through activities specifically designed for a workplace or ministry setting.

The study is structured for groups of leaders to experience together. These "learning groups" can be comprised of intact teams within an organization, church, or ministry—or can be a cohort of leaders from different departments within one organization, or even different organizations altogether. What unites each learning group is each member's desire to get better at leading.

HOW THIS STUDY WORKS:

Week 1 Learning Group Gathering Video & Discussion	**Weeks 2-3** Skills in Action	**Week 4** Now What?

Ideally, five learning group gatherings (one per video session) should be scheduled **at a pace of once per month** over a five-month period, giving you time to practice new leadership skills actively by implementing them in the real world. By spacing your gatherings a month apart, you have time to choose one of the Skills in Action activities (provided) and then engage this new skill between sessions.

Each learning group session takes approximately 90 minutes and includes the key components described below, which help you leverage the principles and practices discussed in its corresponding *Leading from Here to There* video session:

SUGGESTED TIME:
90 minutes

Group Check-In:
15 minutes

Video:
20 minutes

Group Discussion:
45 minutes

My Leadership Challenge:
5 minutes

Session Wrap-Up:
5 minutes

LEARNING GROUP GATHERING

GROUP CHECK-IN:

Session 1 begins with a welcome and introductions. Sessions 2 through 5 begin with 15 minutes dedicated to debriefing the learning group's experience from the previous session, in which they applied one of the Skills In Action activities. Taking time to debrief the previous month's activities not only helps each leader benchmark progress along the way, it also helps fellow group members learn from one another. To discuss your experiences with one another in greater detail, consider extending your debrief time from 15 minutes to 30 minutes. (This will nudge the length of your session closer to two hours.)

VIDEO NOTES:

As you watch the video presentations, use the outline notes to help you focus on the key concepts and principles discussed, writing down anything that stands out to you.

GROUP DISCUSSION:

These questions help you generate insights and foster lively discussion after your group has watched the video. *Throughout this guide, the phrase "your team" is used as a default for applying concepts to your experience. Depending on the scope of your leadership role—whether you lead a team of volunteers, a department of staff members, a process, or a project—feel free to translate "your team" to whatever term would be most appropriate for your situation.*

MY LEADERSHIP CHALLENGE:

At the end of each learning group session, these questions help you focus your learnings and direct you to the specific "Skills In Action Activity" that would be most beneficial for your leadership situation.

SKILLS IN ACTION ACTIVITIES

SKILLS IN ACTION ACTIVITIES:

The Skills in Action activities are designed for you to use with your team back at work or in ministry, or others with whom you work closely. Unless you are doing this study with your work or ministry team, you will not be doing these exercises with your learning group. These activities are a unique feature of this resource—and the key factor in helping you move from head knowledge to skill development. They make your training actionable. True leadership development happens when leaders actually practice what they have learned—and these exercises are tested and proven tools to build your leadership skills.

Maximize your *Leading from Here to There* experience by selecting the activity that will best help your team and sharpen you as a leader. Then accomplish the activity in between sessions. Feel free to tackle more than one activity between sessions—or circle back later and revisit the activities you didn't choose—but that are applicable as you go along.

NOW WHAT?

NOW WHAT:

At the end of each session, a "Now What?" summary wraps up the lesson and provides additional suggestions about how to continue your skill development in this area over the coming months.

You will never regret your decision to invest in yourself as a leader. The apostle Paul challenged leaders in the early church to "lead with all diligence" (Romans 12:8). This includes taking responsibility for developing your leadership gift to its fullest. Your leadership matters. It can change the world.

If you google "leadership," you get more than 640 million hits. If you narrow your search to "definition of leadership," a mere 363 million hits pop up. These simple searches reveal what many leaders feel instinctively: *the topic of leadership is vast and complex*.

Interest in the subject matter of leadership has exploded in the past several decades. Where the subject used to be covered in only a small number of courses within MBA curriculum, today a myriad of academic institutions offer formal degree programs on both the undergraduate and graduate levels. Corporations invest millions in executive education to train their up-and-coming executives in leadership. Every year, thousands of new leadership books hit the consumer market. As any serious leader will attest, the mastery of this subject—if such a thing were even possible—is worthy of a lifetime of learning.

The Leadership Framework - An Organizing Structure

In order to organize this complex subject into more manageable parts, the Willow Creek Association has developed an organizing structure—the Leadership Framework. This framework provides common language, and describes core leadership skills, equipping leaders with a solid foundation upon which to pursue their leadership development.

VISIONARY · SELF · INTERPERSONAL · ORGANIZATIONAL · CALLING

The Leadership Framework

Understanding the Leadership Framework

The key categories of the Leadership Framework are as follows:

- **VISIONARY LEADERSHIP**
  Skills leaders use to move their teams toward a better future.
  The Bible puts it this way: *"Where there is no vision, the people perish"* (Proverbs 29:19, KJV). Visionary leadership topics include: change management, entrepreneurship, innovation, strategy, succession planning, and developing next-generation leaders. In *Leading from Here to There*, Bill Hybels digs into a foundational leadership skill: the team approach to developing a three-to-five-year vision for the future.

- **SELF-LEADERSHIP**
  Skills leaders apply to the most difficult person they will ever lead: themselves.
  According to experts, people who exhibit highly developed self-leadership skills are poised for greater levels of professional and ministry success. Another biblical proverb states, *"Above all else, guard your heart, for everything you do flows from it"* (Proverbs 29:18). Self-leadership topics include: personal spiritual practices, burnout, character, humility, productivity, work/life balance, mental toughness and managing your energy, priorities, and schedule. In this study, Bill Hybels focuses on the leader's need to take responsibility for their own leadership development.

- **INTERPERSONAL LEADERSHIP**
  The people side of leadership.
  In the New Testament, Jesus challenged his followers to be servant leaders— a concept that was a radical reversal for the way leaders acted in his day. Effective leaders navigate relational complexity with truth and grace. Interpersonal leadership topics include: emotional intelligence, leading through influence, bridging generations, empowering volunteers, leveraging situational leadership, conflict resolution, the art of collaboration, and the power of candor. In *Leading From Here to There*, Bill unpacks the concept of 360-degree leadership.

- **ORGANIZATIONAL LEADERSHIP**
  Leading current processes and managing your team day-to-day.
  Effective organizations function well in the practical here-and-now. Jesus described this type of leadership wisdom in a parable found in the gospel of Luke: *"Suppose one of you wants to build a tower. Won't you first sit down and estimate the cost to see if you have enough money to com-*

plete it? For if you lay the foundation and are not able to finish it, everyone who sees it will ridicule you" (Luke 14:28). Organizational leadership topics include: finances, hiring and firing, executing plans or projects, leveraging diversity, decision-making, resource allocation, managing tensions, and crisis management. In this study, Bill unpacks the topic of building a fantastic organizational culture.

o **CALLING**
  The "where" or "why" of leadership.
  While all other elements of the Leadership Framework address the "how" of leadership, the Calling category focuses on the "why." According to Scripture, God has a unique call and purpose for the life of every believer (Ephesians 2:10). If you are a leader, the energy behind your leadership is directed toward a specific issue, need, or cause. This principle applies to every leader, regardless of his or her faith perspective. It answers the question, "What drives you—and why?" Topics in this category include hearing God's "whisper," exploring your strengths, spiritual gifts and "holy discontent," when to engage risk, and living out your calling for the long haul. In this study, Bill engages in a question-and-answer session about how to identify your life's purpose and overcome fear.

As you grow your leadership experience over the next several months, you'll likely identify one or two particular aspects of the Leadership Framework as particular strengths of yours—and identify others where there is more room for growth. Perhaps you excel in interpersonal leadership but are challenged when it comes to self-leadership and self-management. Or maybe you have a visionary, future-oriented leadership style but lack skill in managing day-to-day processes.

Leadership development is a lifelong process. Whether you are just beginning your leadership journey or you've been leading for decades, ask yourself, "Where will I seek to develop my leadership in this season?" When it comes to the vast and complex topic of leadership, you can get better, one step at a time. *Leading from Here to There* can be that next step for you. The world needs your leadership—so dive in!

SESSION 1
THE POWER OF VISION

Vision is a picture of the future that produces passion in people. Leaders must describe a preferred future in graphic, vivid, compelling pictures and statements that would make someone who is comfortable here say to themselves, 'Oh, it would be so much better if we were there.'

—BILL HYBELS

LEARNING GROUP GATHERING

CONVERSATION STARTER (10 minutes)

Welcome to Session 1 of *Leading From Here to There*. If this is your first time together as a learning group, take a few minutes to introduce yourselves before watching the video. Consider sharing:

- Your name
- Your job or ministry role
- Your organization
- When you first realized you were a leader
- What you hope to get out of this leadership study

SESSION

1

**SUGGESTED TIME:
90 minutes**

Welcome/
Conversation Starter:
10 minutes

Video:
30 minutes

Group Discussion:
40 minutes

My Leadership Challenge:
5 minutes

Session Wrap-Up:
5 minutes

VIDEO NOTES: The Power of Vision (30 minutes)

Play the video segment for Session 1. As you watch, use the outline below to follow along or to take notes on anything that stands out to you.

NOTES
Leadership data points

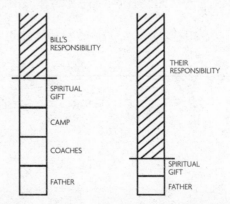

BILL'S RESPONSIBILITY

SPIRITUAL GIFT

CAMP

COACHES

FATHER

THEIR RESPONSIBILITY

SPIRITUAL GIFT

FATHER

It's my responsibility to develop myself as a leader and get better.

Leadership is moving people from here to there.

Sequence:

Begin by building an airtight case for why we cannot stay here.

Vision Leaks

Vision Formation

- o Solo/Sinai Approach

- Team Approach

KEY QUESTION: What does God want our ministry/organization/team to look like three to five years from now?

Vision Affirmation

Vision Declaration

The Power of Vision

GROUP DISCUSSION (40 minutes)

1. Proverbs 29:18 says, *"Where there is no vision, the people perish"* (KJV). In light of this Scripture and the message you just heard from Bill Hybels, how have you experienced vision (or lack of vision) in your business or ministry life?

2. Whenever leaders discuss vision, it is helpful to start by defining terms. Read the definitions below. Discuss with your learning group your understanding about the differences between Mission and Vision.

> ### DEFINING TERMS
>
> Sometimes people think mission and vision are the same thing. They are two distinct pieces of a team or organization's guiding framework.
>
> **Mission** is a simple statement of what you do. It is your core competence. Generally, your mission doesn't change over time.
>
> **Vision** is a future-oriented, challenging, and exciting statement about where your team, ministry, business, or organization wants to go. It will change over time—typically every three to five years for a team or longer for a larger organization.

3. Has your team* formed, affirmed, and declared a vision? If yes, how did you accomplish the vision process? If no, what barriers will you face in establishing a vision with your team?

> THE SOVEREIGN LORD DOES NOTHING WITHOUT
> # REVEALING HIS PLAN
> TO HIS SERVANTS.
>
> AMOS 3:7

---

* Throughout this guide, the phrase "your team" is used as a default for applying concepts to your experience. Depending on the scope of your leadership role—whether you lead a team of volunteers, a department of staff members, a process, or a project—feel free to translate "your team" to whatever term would be most appropriate for your situation.

4. Forming vision is best done as a team. But often the process starts in the mind of the leader. Take the next 10 minutes to individually reflect on how you might answer Bill's key question: "What does God want our ministry/organization/team to look like three to five years from now?" Use the questions below to help guide your thinking. Write down your answers and share your insights with your learning group.

- What changes do you anticipate internally within your team over the next three to five years?

- What external changes (technology, demographics, customer needs, expansion, contraction) do you see coming in the next three to five years that will affect the work your team does?

- What will those you serve need or want from you that they aren't getting today?

○ What will those you serve no longer need or want?

5. Who could you consult to validate or challenge your thoughts regarding the changes coming to your team? How could you involve your team in the process?

MY LEADERSHIP CHALLENGE (5 minutes)
Vision Formation

As you close your learning group time, take the last 5 minutes to consider your personal takeaway(s) and select the Skills in Action Activity you will work on from this session.

6. My top two personal takeaways are:

1

2

7. Identify the action step that will most help your team move forward in understanding and implementing your vision. Check the box that most accurately reflects the current state of vision on your team. The box you select will help you identify the Skills in Action Activity that would be most applicable for your leadership situation.

   ❑ Our current vision statement may not reflect where we need to go in the next three to five years. It may be time to rework it.
   (Skills in Action: Evaluate Your Vision, p. 28)

   ❑ We do not yet have a clearly identified vision statement for our team.
   (Skills in Action: Form Your Vision, p. 29)

   ❑ We have a clearly identified vision statement but have not done the work to get affirmation or buy-in from others in our organization.
   (Skills in Action: Affirm Your Vision, p. 31)

   ❑ Our current vision statement is accurate, but the words don't really produce passion in people.
   (Skills in Action: Put Language to Your Vision, p. 33)

   ❑ I understand the vision of my organization and team but would like to gain greater clarity on a vision for my individual role.
   (Skills in Action: Develop a Vision for Your Individual Role, p. 35)

8. My Skills in Action is: _____

   o Share the activity you selected with your learning group.

SESSION WRAP-UP

Close your time in prayer together, asking God to help each member to grow in the leadership skill of vision in the coming month.

The real power of this study comes as you apply the concepts you discussed in your learning group to your real-life teams at work or in ministry.

Read through the five Skills in Action for visionary leadership on the pages that follow and select the activity that will help your team move forward in understanding and living their vision. For some of you, these might be new experiences. Practicing new skills can feel awkward at first, but know that your team will be stronger and more focused after completing these activities. As you take responsibility for your own growth in your leadership, your ability to help a team or organization form, affirm, and declare a vision will be vital tools in your leadership toolbox.

SKILLS IN ACTION ACTIVITIES
SESSION 1: The Power of Vision

Leaders move people and projects *From Here to There*. They sense something is wrong about "here"—and can envision a better future ahead if only they can get people to go "there"! King Solomon of Israel—renowned throughout history for his wise leadership—understood the vital importance of vision when he penned these famous words: *"Where there is no vision, the people perish"* (Proverbs 29:19, KJV). Bill Hybels defines vision as "a picture of the future that produces passion in people."

Establishing vision is best done as a team. Direction that a leader senses is the right way to go—or even divinely inspired "whispers" from God—are best affirmed by a team, not by one leader alone. This type of vision formation can be time-intensive, but the payoff comes when your entire team feels affirmed and valued in the process. They gain clarity, focus, and renewed energy in their unique roles and contributions.

If you are more of an individual contributor whose leadership focuses around projects or processes, clarifying your vision for the scope of your leadership is still important. Clearly articulating where your process or project needs to go in the future—and then gaining alignment and support from others involved—is essential to leading change of any kind.

The Skills in Action activities on the following pages are tested processes to help your team, back at work or in ministry, with vision formation and affirmation. Unless you are doing this study as a team, these activities are not intended for you to do with your learning group. Read the Skills in Action Activity descriptions and select one that you will accomplish in the next month. All the activities can also be done by an individual contributor by substituting "my project/process" anywhere you see "my team" in the questions. Leaders are built when they actualize the training they receive. The key is to take action!

SKILLS IN ACTION ACTIVITIES:
The Power of Vision

If your team has never done a vision process, if you are in a time of transition, or if it has been a while since you have visited this topic, try the following sequence.

1. Evaluate Your Vision

2. Form Your Vision

3. Affirm Your Vision

4. Put Language to Your Vision

(Develop a Vision for Your Individual Role is done outside the team context.)

Evaluate Your Vision   PAGE 28

This exercise allows you to evaluate a vision's relevance and effectiveness.

Form Your Vision   PAGE 29

If your team has never developed a vision—or if it has been more than three to five years since your team has gone through this process—use this approach to help your team discern and form a fresh and compelling vision.

Affirm Your Vision   PAGE 31

If your team has recently formed a vision, this activity will help you "shop the vision" to gain input and alignment from key stakeholders on your vision.

Put Language to Your Vision   PAGE 33

Use this approach to put words to your vision by writing a succinct vision statement. This exercise helps you paint "a picture of the future that produces passion in people."

Develop a Vision for
Your Individual Role   PAGE 35

If you exercise your leadership by leading processes and projects, this activity helps you develop a vision for your unique role.

VISIONARY

Self

Interpersonal

Organizational

Calling

SKILLS IN ACTION
Evaluate Your Vision

Make it a practice to evaluate your vision on a regular basis to account for changing realities both within and outside of your team. If it has been a year or more since you evaluated the relevance of your vision, this activity will help your team work through the process.

Make a copy of your team's current vision and mission statements and your organization's vision and mission statements (if applicable).

Gather your team for a team discussion and ask the following questions:

- What is our current reality?

    - What were the current realities when we originally drafted this vision?

    - What has changed? What are our new current realities?

    - Is our vision still valid, given our realities today?

    - How does our team's mission and vision support the mission and vision of our organization. Pass out the mission and vision statement and be sure your team understands the difference between mission and vision (page 21).

- Is our vision aligned with that of the broader organization?

- Does our current vision statement provide a picture of the future that produces passion in people?

If, after your discussion, the team's consensus is that the vision is outdated or no longer valid, rework your vision with the team using one of the approaches outlined in Skills in Action: Develop Your Team's Vision, Skills in Action: Affirm Your Vision, or Skills In Action: Put Language to Your Vision.

This activity generally takes about 30 minutes to one hour, depending on the size of your team and the depth of your conversation.

 Once you have completed your activity, go to Now What? on page 37 for additional ideas, next steps, and resources.

SKILLS IN ACTION
Form Your Vision

Use this approach if your team has new members, has not worked together for very long, or is unclear about goals and objectives.

Gather your team together to discuss the questions outlined below. To engage everyone on the team and develop a greater sense of ownership for the vision, use flip charts posted around the room with the questions below written at the top—and then ask team members to write their answers directly on the chart (or onto sticky notes they place on the charts). Assign a team member to each chart, and ask that team member to present all the comments or ideas submitted by your team.

Before you start, go back to the Mission and Vision definition on page 21 to be sure that everyone understands the terms.

Look Back

- How would we plot the history of our team? When was it formed and who was present? (Try to answer what you can even if it pre-dates your leadership.)

- How would we describe various stages of maturity for our team?

- What have been some of the highs for our team throughout our history?

- What have been some of the lows for our team throughout our history?

Look at Current State ("Here")

- What unique value or gift does our team provide to those we serve today?

- Who is the primary target audience for our team's services?

- What strengths does our team possess (e.g., skills, knowledge, processes)?

- How does our team's mission and vision support the mission and vision of our organization?

- What weaknesses present challenges to our team (e.g., staffing, physical plant, finances, external barriers, culture)?

- What is good about *here*—the product or service we provide? How are we making a difference?

- Why can't we stay *here*, providing the product or service the way we do today? What needs are we missing, what is not working, or what is confusing about what we are doing today?

Look Forward

- What is changing in the next three to five years surrounding the work that we do? (Think about changes both inside and outside our team— e.g., changes with customers, staff, the broader organization, processes, technology, the larger community, or society as a whole).

- How will changes in these areas affect what we do?

- What will those we serve need or want that they don't get from us today?

- What will those we serve no longer need or want from us?

- **KEY QUESTION:** What does God want our team/organization/ministry to look like three to five years from now?

Draft Your Vision

- How would you describe the next phase of your team? What one-word label would you give it? What would be the tag line?

- Take a stab at writing a vision statement. Use the guidance for writing a vision statement shared in Skills In Action: Putting Language to Your Vision.

This activity can take from three to four hours or more, depending on the size of your team and depth of the conversation. It can also be divided up into two or four separate meetings. Alternatively, some teams choose to spend a weekend retreat working through these exercises.

 Once you have completed your activity, go to Now What? on page 37 for additional ideas, next steps, and resources.

SKILLS IN ACTION
Affirm Your Vision

The first thing a leader needs to do once the team's vision has been crafted is to seek input and alignment with key stakeholders within (and possibly outside) the team. Bill called this "shopping your vision." Inviting those who depend on—or have a stake in—your team's work to speak into your vision and share input creates more buy-in and support for your team and the direction you are heading (your vision). It also protects your team from pursuing endeavors that the organization will not support because they don't align with the direction of the broader organization.

Gather your team to discuss, prioritize, and plan for stakeholder meetings to get input and reactions to your vision. You may want to also bring along your organization's mission statement and the definitions on page 21 to be sure your stakeholders understand the bigger picture of how your new vision fits into the larger mission of your organization.

1. Start your discussion by listing your stakeholders and how you think they will respond to your vision.

STAKEHOLDER	(+) ANTICIPATE POSITIVE REACTIONS	(0) ANTICIPATE NEUTRAL REACTIONS	(-) ANTICIPATE HESITANT OR CONCERNED REACTIONS

2. Ask your team which stakeholders they feel are the highest priority to meet with for input—and why. Take into consideration how much influence each stakeholder can have either to support or delay your vision achievement.

3. Make a plan to meet with prioritized stakeholders that includes details on who will meet with each one, by when, what questions will be asked and what materials will be used to communicate.

Gather your team after all the stakeholder meetings have been completed to share the feedback collected. Discuss how you will (or will not) incorporate the feedback and make plans to adjust your vision accordingly.

This activity can take between one and four hours, depending on the number of stakeholders with whom you choose to meet.

 Once you have completed your activity, go to Now What? on page 37 for additional ideas, next steps, and resources.

SKILLS IN ACTION
Put Language to Your Vision

This activity helps your team put language to a vision you already have identified but haven't yet captured in words—or helps you refine your existing wording to create a vision that is more clear and inspiring.

Vision is a picture of the future that produces passion in people. Vision statements are ambitious and aspirational in nature. They evoke emotion and inspire hope and confidence about where the team or organization is headed. Although vision involves dreaming about the future, it must be rooted in the purpose—or mission—of the team.

Vision statements typically include the following components:

Future Achievement	Expected Results
A description of a future achievement that is ambitious and challenging	A description of the expected outcome of the achievement, something that answers "in order to _____" or "so that_____"

It explains why the future achievement matters and what difference it will make.

Example of visions that have been achieved:

Ford Motor Company in the early 1900s:
We will democratize the automobile so that everyone will be able to afford one and everyone will have one.

Example of visions in process:

Willow Creek Association:
Helping Christians grow their leadership [in order] to maximize kingdom impact.

Gather your team for a brainstorm meeting on vision language.

1. Begin by passing out your team's mission and vision statements—along with the definitions on page 21. If your team is part of a larger organization, also pass out your organization's mission and vision statements. Discuss:

   o how your team's mission supports the larger organization's mission;

   o how your team's vision supports the larger organization's vision;

   o why a new vision statement—a picture of the future that produces passion in people—could be helpful for your team.

2. Ahead of time, draw two columns on a white board or flip chart and label them "Future Achievement" and "Expected Result." Appoint a scribe to capture everyone's language in the columns.

3. Ask everyone individually to write on a card how they would describe your team's future achievement in a way that is inspiring and challenging. The achievement should use a verb and a noun that succinctly describe the central mission of your team.

4. Ask them to write on a second card what the expected result or the future aspiration would be. The result should be described with inspiring language to show how accomplishing your three-to-five year vision will make a difference.

5. When everyone is finished, ask each team member to share their statements with the group, as the scribe captures each statement in the columns.

6. Spend the rest of your meeting merging the language of the statements that your team created. Give yourself a time limit. At the end of the time, you should be close to having a clear, compelling, accurate vision statement that captures your team's aspirations and expected outcomes. You may need to schedule another meeting to tweak the language further, or you may assign that task to one or two people who will report back to the team.

This activity generally takes between one and two hours, depending on the size of your team and the depth of your conversation.

 Once you have completed your activity, go to Now What? on page 37 for additional ideas, next steps, and resources.

SKILLS IN ACTION
Develop a Vision for Your Individual Role

When you have a clear, compelling vision for your individual work or ministry role—taking into account changing market or ministry considerations—you gain clarity on your priorities, upcoming challenges, and where your role might be heading in the future.

Schedule a time with your supervisor to discuss your vision and goals. Having honest conversations about where your role might be headed in the future ensures that both of you are headed in the same direction. Alignment with your supervisor makes it more likely that you will be able to reach your goals.

Before your meeting, take some time to write out your thoughts about the questions below.

- What are your greatest highs and lows in your current ministry or work role to date?

- What is your key competency as a professional?

- In your current role, are you under-challenged, over-challenged, or appropriately challenged?

- What changes do you foresee in the next three to five years surrounding the work that you do—and how will those changes affect you?

- Pray and consider: Where may God be asking you to go professionally in the next three to five years?

- Take a stab at writing a preliminary personal vision statement using guidance from Skills In Action: Put Language to Your Vision.

During the meeting with your supervisor, share the key insights you uncovered in your reflection time. Ask for input on how your supervisor envisions your future—and work to gain alignment about your vision, goals, and opportunities in the future.

This activity generally takes between one and two hours, depending on the depth of your reflection and the length of time of your supervisor meeting.

 Once you have completed your activity, go to Now What? on page 37 for additional ideas, next steps, and resources.

NOW WHAT?

Forming a vision with your team is a powerful step in moving people from here to there. Begin by gaining support and buy-in from those closest to the work you are doing. The engagement and ownership of your team in developing the vision will be exponentially higher than if you had developed your vision on your own. Now that you have completed one Skills in Action Activity, you may find it applicable to move on to other activities from this session.

Once you have identified and put language to your vision, declaring your vision is a critical next step. The worst thing a team can do after they have crafted a vision is hang it on the wall or put it in a drawer. You should plan to communicate your team's vision to anyone who needs to support and contribute to the vision achievement. You may want to think of creative ways to begin every meeting by stating the vision—especially for the first few months. When your team knows your vision by heart and is tired of hearing you repeat it, you know they have internalized the message.

> WHEN YOUR TEAM **KNOWS YOUR VISION** BY HEART AND IS TIRED OF HEARING **YOU REPEAT IT,** YOU KNOW THEY HAVE **INTERNALIZED THE MESSAGE.**

Think carefully through a communication plan that will inspire others to work toward your vision with you. If you require only a small number of people to achieve your vision, periodic meetings may be all that is needed to keep the vision white-hot. If it will take a large number of individuals to achieve your vision, you may need multiple methods of communication and high-frequency contact with them in order to help the vision stick and keep it fresh in everyone's mind.

Often, crafting the vision is the easy part. The hard work comes in making your vision come to life and achieving it over time. In essence, this is the role of a leader—moving people from *here* to *there*.

My Action Plan – The Power of Vision

Use the chart below to plan your next steps for developing a vision. Do you need to do a more in-depth vision exercise with your team? Do you need to "shop your vision" or rewrite your statement with more inspiring language? Or is it time to declare your vision? Write your next step in the chart below—thinking through a realistic deadline and other people you will need to include in your plan.

Next Step	By When	Who should I include?	Who could help or coach me?

THE TOUGHEST PERSON YOU LEAD

> Earlier in my leadership career, I felt it was someone else's job to develop me. Somehow, I eventually broke through that victim mentality, and I said to myself, **'For the rest of my life, if nobody develops me, I'm still going to develop myself.'** That's a watershed mark in the life of a leader.

—BILL HYBELS

LEARNING GROUP GATHERING

CHECK-IN (15 minutes)

Welcome to Session 2 of *Leading From Here to There*. A key part of learning any new skill is getting input from fellow learners. Before watching the video, debrief your Skills in Action experience from Session 1: The Power of Vision. Use the following questions to guide your discussion.

- Which Skills in Action Activity did you complete?
- What was the experience like for you?
- What was the impact on your team?
- What do you see as next steps to continue to develop or implement your vision?

SUGGESTED TIME:
90 minutes

Check-In:
15 minutes

Video:
20 minutes

Group Discussion:
45 minutes

My Leadership Challenge:
5 minutes

Session Wrap-Up:
5 minutes

VIDEO NOTES: The Toughest Person You Lead (20 minutes)

Play the video segment for Session 2. As you watch, use the outline below to follow along or to take notes.

NOTES

The concept of "360-degree leadership" was first developed by Dee Hock, a renowned leadership expert and the founder of the Visa Credit Card company.

The toughest person you will ever lead is *you*.

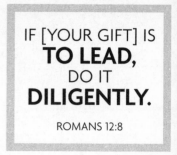

IF [YOUR GIFT] IS
TO LEAD,
DO IT
DILIGENTLY.

ROMANS 12:8

Take responsibility for your own leadership development.

How do you get better as a leader?

1. Read everything you can read on the subject matter of leadership.

YOU DON'T HAVE TO
KNOW
SOMEONE TO BE
MENTORED
BY THEM.

2. Go where leadership is taught.

3. Find people ahead of you in leadership and ask them smart questions.

4. Lead with greater intensity tomorrow than you did today.

5. Keep a leadership journal as a discipline.

BUILD
YOURSELVES UP
IN FAITH...
JUDE 20 (MSG)

GROUP DISCUSSION (45 minutes)

1. In Romans 12:8, Paul says, *"If [your gift] is to lead, do it diligently."* How do you see that verse applying to your leadership—in light of the way Bill Hybels described self-leadership in his message?

2. Bill described a watershed mark where he realized he was the one ultimately responsible for his own leadership development. In what ways can you identify with this pivotal moment? In what areas of development are you still expecting someone else to take the initiative for you?

3. Bill said that we should lead with greater intensity every day, knowing that much of our development happens on-the-job. Experts say, for most people, 70% of development should happen on the job through experience, 20% should happen through relationships with feedback and coaching, and 10% should happen through formal learning methods like training programs, degree programs, certifications or reading (Center for Creative Leadership).

Using the self-assessment diagram below, estimate how your leadership development happens today and identify where adjustments might be made to optimize your on-the-job learning. When you have finished with your self-assessment, share your insights with your learning group.

DEVELOPMENT EXAMPLES

On the Job	Relationships	Learning Methods
70%	**20%**	**10%**
○ Take on new responsibilities	○ Seek feedback from others	○ Read as a discipline
○ Substitute for your supervisor on a task or in a meeting	○ Develop a mentoring relationship	○ Watch TED Talks or podcasts
○ Participate in a group to solve a problem	○ Interview a leader ahead of you	○ Attend training programs or conferences
○ Improve a process and implement the change	○ Leverage your experience by teaching others	○ Obtain a degree or certification

WHERE I AM CURRENTLY DEVELOPING MY LEADERSHIP

On the Job	Relationships	Learning Methods
_____ %	_____ %	_____ %
Examples	Examples	Examples
❑ _____	❑ _____	❑ _____
❑ _____	❑ _____	❑ _____
❑ _____	❑ _____	❑ _____

4. Bill talked about finding leaders ahead of you in leadership and asking them smart questions. He shared his example of interviewing Bob Galvin from Motorola. If you have had a similar experience, share it with your learning group. If you haven't, what obstacles do you face in seeking out a more experienced leader?

5. Identify one or two leaders in your community whom you would like to interview. Share with your learning group.

6. Bill said we need to reflect periodically on how we are doing at treasuring the people under our leadership. He described keeping a leadership journal as a discipline. A leadership journal is kept for the specific purpose of monitoring your leadership—separate and distinct from a spiritual reflection journal. Have you kept such a leadership journal? If yes, how does it help you? If no, what are your thoughts about Bill's advice to start one?

MY LEADERSHIP CHALLENGE (5 minutes)
Developing My Leadership

As you close your learning group time, take the last 5 minutes to consider your personal takeaway(s) and select the Skills in Action Activity you will work on from this session.

7. My top two personal takeaways are:

1	

2	

8. Identify the development activity(ies) that would be most beneficial toward helping you grow your self-leadership over the next month. The box you select will help you select the Skills in Action Activity that would make the biggest impact on your leadership development.

- ❏ Keep a leadership journal for reflection and assessment
  (Skills in Action: Keep a Leadership Journal as a Discipline, p. 48)

- ❏ Read books about leadership
  (Skills in Action: The Reading Challenge, p. 50)

- ❏ Interview a more experienced leader
  (Skills in Action: Conduct a Leadership Interview, p. 51)

- ❏ Take on new on-the-job leadership challenges or assignments
  (Skills in Action: Lead with Greater Intensity/On-the-Job Challenge, p. 52)

9. My Skills in Action is: _____

- o Share the activity you selected with your learning group.

SESSION WRAP-UP

Close your time in prayer together, asking God to help each member to grow in the skill of self-leadership in the next month.

If you have experienced a watershed moment like Bill described, you know that you need to take responsibility for your own leadership development. It will take time and intention, but it will also have enormous impact on your effectiveness. Read through the four Skills in Action activities, get out your calendar, and make a plan to accomplish at least one over the next month.

SKILLS IN ACTION ACTIVITIES
SESSION 2: The Toughest Person You Lead

When most of us think about leadership, we think about "leading down" to the people on our teams or those "below us" on an organizational chart. But, counterintuitively, the toughest person you lead is actually the one you see in the mirror every day—you!

According to experts, highly developed self-leadership skills are actually one of the biggest factors in professional success. When we take responsibility for our own leadership development, we open ourselves up for greater impact.

In addressing first-century church leaders in Rome, the apostle Paul encouraged them to "lead with all diligence" (Romans 12:8). Leading with "all diligence" means we need to take responsibility for using our leadership gifts to their fullest. The impact one leader can have for good or evil in our society is enormous. All you have to do is look around you at work, in your community, or in our world and you will see the evidence of poor leadership and good leadership. In the midst of all the ups and downs of leadership, be sure that you do not waver on developing your leadership abilities.

There are many ways you can develop yourself as a leader. Read through the Skills in Action activities in the pages that follow and select one or two that you will accomplish in the next month. Take responsibility by taking action on your own self-development—starting now!

SKILLS IN ACTION ACTIVITIES:
The Toughest Person You Lead

**Keep a Leadership
Journal as a Discipline** PAGE 48

This activity gets you started in keeping a leadership journal by
identifying ten key questions to help you periodically reflect on
your leadership.

The Reading Challenge PAGE 50

This activity encourages you to identify a leadership book to read
over the next month.

Conduct a Leadership Interview PAGE 51

Use this approach to identify and interview one leader in your
community who is ahead of you and whom you admire.

**Lead with Greater Intensity/
On-the-Job Challenge** PAGE 52

This exercise prepares you to engage your supervisor in
conversations about on-the-job growth opportunities that
can help you develop as a leader.

Visionary

SELF

Interpersonal

Organizational

Calling

SKILLS IN ACTION
Keep a Leadership Journal as a Discipline

Bill suggested that leaders keep a journal specifically about their own leadership—and that they should write in it during regular intervals as a discipline. Begin by identifying ten questions you need to ask to reflect on your leadership regularly—say, once per month or once per quarter. Take time now to write out these questions so you can engage in an initial reflection on your leadership. Carry the journal with you throughout your week so you can regularly reflect on significant leadership moments. Consider starting a new leadership journal at the beginning of each year.

Use the following topic list along with Bill's first two questions in the chart that follows to identify the ten questions you will reflect on regularly. Include thought-provoking questions that will give you insight and help you assess your self-leadership. Some categories you might consider include:

- Spiritual disciplines
- Rest and replenishment cycles
- State of key relationships
- Conflict management
- Financial discipline

- Physical activity
- Calendar alignment to priorities
- Heart of compassion
- Treasuring people
- State of my personal integrity

1	Am I getting better as a leader? In what ways?
2	Am I inspiring the people God has entrusted to me? How would I know?
3	
4	
5	
6	
7	
8	
9	
10	

After you have identified your top ten questions, take time in the coming month to journal about each question. What did your reflections reveal about your current leadership strengths? Areas that need development?

Finish this exercise by taking out your calendar and scheduling a regular time, once each month or each quarter, to step away from your busy leadership schedule and journal your current answers to the ten questions, as a discipline. Encourage yourself by reviewing your growth over time.

This activity can take between one and two hours, depending on the depth of your reflection.

 Once you have completed your activity, go to Now What? on page 56 for additional ideas, next steps, and resources.

SKILLS IN ACTION
The Reading Challenge

Identify a leadership book that you will commit to read as a discipline over the next month. Consider asking one to three other people to read the same book. Upon completing the book, journal your answers to the questions below. If you are reading with others, schedule a brief time to discuss your answers to these questions.

- What is the main idea of the book?

- How was your thinking challenged by the author?

- What one or two tangible concepts from the book can you implement?

If you found this exercise helpful, consider challenging yourself with a bigger goal to read one leadership book each month over a twelve-month period.

Below is a list of just a few leadership books Bill recommends. Some are on leadership as a broad topic, while others drill into specific, critical leadership skills. (Note: This list is not exhaustive; it is simply provided as a way to get you started on building an excellent leadership library.)

Leadership	Specific Leadership Skills	Leader Biographies
• *The Effective Executive*, Peter F. Drucker	• *Crucial Conversations*, Kerry Patterson & Joseph Grenny	• *Team of Rivals*, Doris Kearns Goodwin
• *Good to Great*, Jim Collins	• *Thanks for the Feedback*, Doug Stone & Sheila Heen	• *No Higher Honor*, Condoleezza Rice
• *The Intangibles of Leadership*, Richard Davis	• *The Five Dysfunctions of a Team*, Patrick Lencioni	• *My American Journey*, Colin Powell
• *Primal Leadership*, Daniel Goleman	• *Daring Greatly*, Brené Brown	• *Tough Choices*, Carly Fiorina
• *Winning*, Jack Welch	• *Leading Change*, John Kotter	• *Eyewitness to Power*, David Gergen
	• *Multipliers*, Liz Wiseman	

This activity can take between one and eight hours, depending on your reading speed.

 Once you have completed your activity, go to Now What? on page 56 for additional ideas, next steps, and resources.

SKILLS IN ACTION
Conduct a Leadership Interview

Identify and interview one leader in your community whom you admire and from whom you would like to learn. When requesting a meeting, consider using an opening line like Bill's: "I really respect what you've built. May I buy you lunch?" Commit to the leader that you will only take 30–60 minutes of her time and will come prepared with three specific questions. Prepare for the interview by making sure the questions are: 1) most critical for your leadership right now, 2) an area about which that leader might have some insight, and 3) not something you could have learned yourself by reading what the leader has already written about/spoken on, etc.

List your three questions:

1.

2.

3.

After you conduct the interview, write down your insights in your leadership journal.

o   What did the leader say that surprised you?

o   What advice did the leader share?

o   How did the leader challenge your thinking?

o   What will you do differently as a result of what you learned during the interview?

This activity can take between one and three hours, depending on the depth of your reflection and note taking. Don't worry if you can't get a meeting within the next thirty days—you can debrief with your learning group in a future meeting.

 Once you have completed your activity, go to Now What? on page 56 for additional ideas, next steps, and resources.

SKILLS IN ACTION
Lead with Greater Intensity/On-the-Job Challenge

In this session, Bill said that leaders should aspire to lead with greater intensity every day because much of their development happens on the job. In the group discussion, you were introduced to the concept that 70% of your development typically happens through on-the-job experience. Classroom learning can only take you so far. You develop most quickly when you throw yourself into a new situation and need to figure it out.

This exercise prepares you to engage your supervisor in conversations about on-the-job growth opportunities that can help you develop as a leader.

STEP ONE: REFLECTION
Take time to reflect about on the developmental experiences in which you might want to engage at your current job over the next six to twelve months. Use the questions below to guide your thinking.

1. Below are some examples of common on-the-job development experiences. Highlight or circle the ones that seem interesting or relevant for your situation. Feel free to add others.

PRACTICAL EXAMPLES FOR ON-THE-JOB DEVELOPMENTAL EXPERIENCES

Expand Your Responsibilities

- Take on these new responsibilities:

- Substitute for your supervisor in leading a task or a meeting.

- Assume managerial responsibilities for a team.

- Increase decision-making authority.

- Increase the number of processes, projects, or departments you manage.

- Other: _____

Solve Problems

- Participate in a short-term task force to solve an organizational problem.

- Tackle a problem or a process that is not working by getting feedback from coworkers or a more experienced leader and trying a new approach.

- Introduce new or innovative approaches to your current work process.

- Apply a disciplined problem-solving approach such as Six Sigma* to a current problem.

Try New Experiences

- Cover for a coworker on leave.

- Join a project team or committee in a different area of the organization.

- Be purposeful about increasing your interaction with stakeholders you typically don't engage—such as donors, potential customers, volunteers, senior management, or board members.

- Take part in types of work you haven't done before, such as giving presentations, helping with budgeting, or interviewing potential new team members.

2. Next, think about your ministry or organization. Outside of your current role and areas of responsibilities, what other projects, departments, or roles interest you? Or within your current role, what need could you meet or expanded responsibility could you take on, which would stretch your skillset in new ways? List seven interest areas on the next page and describe how each might stretch you.

---

* Six Sigma is a data-driven methodology to reduce defects and improve performance of a process. Six Sigma is widely used in manufacturing settings but has become more mainstream in application to business processes, whether operational or service oriented in nature. Learn more at *sixsigmaonline.org*.

Projects, Roles, or Expanded Responsibilities	How It Might Stretch Me
1.	
2.	
3.	
4.	
5.	
6.	
7.	

3. Go back to your highlights in Question 1 and your list in Question 2. Narrow the list down to four development options that you could suggest to your supervisor as an on-the-job growth plan for you over the next six to twelve months?

My Top Four

1

2

3

4

STEP TWO: MEET WITH YOUR SUPERVISOR

Meet with your supervisor and/or a mentor to talk through your on-the-job development. Present your top four options and discuss which one or two might be the most viable for you over the next twelve months.

STEP THREE: TRY SOMETHING NEW ON THE JOB

If you have an opportunity, with your supervisor's approval, try something new on-the-job. Write down some reflections on how it went and prepare to share with your learning group.

This activity can take between one and two hours, depending on the depth of your reflection, the amount of time you meet with your supervisor, and the new experience you try.

 Once you have completed your activity, go to Now What? on page 56 for additional ideas, next steps, and resources.

NOW WHAT?

Changing behavior, whether your own or someone else's, takes time. If you tried a new behavior this month, and it felt difficult to you, don't be discouraged. The more you work at becoming intentional in developing yourself as a leader, the more natural it will feel. Now that you've completed one of the Skills in Action activities, you may want to try another. Be sure to take time to identify how your learnings apply on your job. Set goals and include others who can help you stay accountable to applying what you've learned.

> ## IT'S UP TO YOU
> —AND NO ONE ELSE—
> ## TO PROACTIVELY
> PURSUE YOUR
> OWN GROWTH.

Leadership development is never done. Circumstances change, people change, settings change, markets change, and the scope and scale of your role will change. The revolving dynamics around you necessitate continued leadership growth. Much of what you need to learn costs nothing and is available to you on the job. Keeping a leadership journal as a discipline and setting regular goals for development can be the spark for your development. Keep learning throughout the year by reading leadership books, attending seminars, and taking on new assignments in your work or ministry role. Make sure you vary your development experiences.

But remember: you need to take responsibility for your own leadership development. It's up to you—and no one else—to proactively pursue your own growth. Take the apostle Paul's words to the leaders in Rome to heart—and lead with all diligence!

My Action Plan – The Toughest Person You Lead

Use the chart below to plan your next steps in self-leadership. Do you want to try interviewing a leader in your community or developing a book reading plan? Maybe you would like to attend a conference or a course—or become involved in a new project that will stretch you at work or in ministry. Write your next step in the chart below—thinking through a realistic deadline and other people you will need to include in your plan.

Next Step	By When	Who should I include?	Who could help or coach me?

MASTERING 360-DEGREE LEADERSHIP

> Most of us need to get better in managing our leadership relationships. Some of us lead *down* pretty well, but we have sharp elbows and don't lead well *laterally*. Or some of us lead well *laterally*, but we've just never thought about how to lead *up*. Over time, you will begin to feel a certain level of comfort in leading up, leading laterally, and leading down. That's when it feels like **nothing is better than the privilege of leadership**.
>
> —BILL HYBELS

LEARNING GROUP GATHERING

GROUP CHECK-IN (15 minutes)

Welcome to Session 3 of *Leading From Here to There*. A key part of learning any new skill is getting input from fellow learners. Debrief your self-leadership Skills in Action experience from Session 2: Self-Leadership with your learning group. Use the following questions to guide your discussion.

- Which Skills in Action Activity did you complete?
- What was the experience like for you?
- What are your most vital next steps to help you continue developing your self-leadership?

VIDEO NOTES: Mastering 360-Degree Leadership (25 minutes)

Play the video segment for Session 3. As you watch, use the outline below to follow along or to take notes.

SUGGESTED TIME:
90 minutes

Group Check-In:
15 minutes

Video:
25 minutes

Group Discussion:
40 minutes

My Leadership Challenge:
5 minutes

Session Wrap-Up:
5 minutes

NOTES

360-Degree Leadership

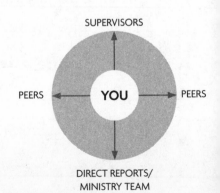

Leading Down

> THE RULERS OF THE GENTILES
> LORD IT OVER THEM...
> **NOT SO WITH YOU.**
> INSTEAD, WHOEVER
> WANTS TO BECOME
> GREAT AMONG
> YOU MUST BE
> **YOUR SERVANT.**
> MATTHEW 20:25–26

Fantastic people are hard to find

- Character

- Competence

THE FIVE C'S

CHARACTER

COMPETENCE

CHEMISTRY

CULTURE*

CALLING*

- Chemistry

* Bill will cover the topic of
Culture in Session 4 and
Calling in Session 5.

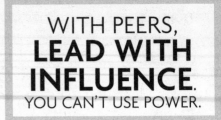

Leading Up

To influence your supervisor:

o   Be a super performer.

o   Consider the timing.

o   Use a spirit of respect.

GROUP DISCUSSION (40 minutes)

1. In Matthew 20:25–26, Jesus called his disciples to assume a posture of servant leadership in all of their relationships. What stood out to you from Bill's talk? How do you see the principle of servant leadership applying to your 360-degree relationships?

2. Bill suggested you assess where you are in leading laterally, leading up, and leading down. Use the chart below to list your 360-Degree Relationships visually. Then, using symbols, such as a plus sign, minus sign or check mark, indicate the strength of the relationships:

+	✓	—
Strong Relationship	Neutral Relationship	Negative or Weak Relationship

Sample Relationship Map

UP	Andy +	Jane +	Irina ✓	Troy ✓	Chris +
LATERAL	Leslie −	Dan −	YOU	Deb −	Tim ✓
DOWN	John +	Nate +	Diane ✓	David ✓	

My Map

UP	
LATERAL	YOU
DOWN	

What patterns stand out as you review your map?

3. What can you do to invest purposefully in your neutral and negative relationships?

4. Bill suggested creating and sustaining your team according to Character, Competence, Chemistry. Think about your team.

   o Which one of these C's is strongest on your team?

   o Which one of these has the most potential for improvement?

   o Brainstorm with your learning group to come up with some concrete ways you can improve the C you identified above.

5. Bill said that good lateral leadership involves leading through influence—not through power. From your own experience, add to the two lists that follow: one that describes the characteristics of strong lateral leadership practices and one that describes the characteristics of poor lateral leadership practices. Discuss your lists with your learning group.

Strong Lateral Leadership Practices	Poor Lateral Leadership Practices
o Teammates sacrifice their own agenda to help others.	o Teammates are self-involved.
o Teams give up status/budget for the greater good.	o Teams are siloed and go against each other for resources.
o	o
o	o
o	o
o	o

In your organization, what are the barriers to good lateral leadership?

6. Mark on the scale below to indicate how secure you feel in speaking candidly to those above you in your organization. To the degree you are comfortable, share your response—and how you might grow in this area, if needed.

1 _____ 5

I feel extremely uncomfortable having candid conversations with leaders above me.

I am very comfortable having candid conversations with leaders above me.

7. Discuss Bill's three suggestions for leading up. How might you increase your effectiveness in these areas?

o Be a super performer.

o Consider the timing.

o Use a spirit of respect.

MY LEADERSHIP CHALLENGE (5 minutes)
Developing a Plan to Grow in 360-Degree Leadership

As you close your learning group time, take the last 5 minutes to consider your personal takeaway(s) and select the Skills in Action Activity that you will work on from this session.

8. My top two personal takeaways are:

1	

2	

9. In which of the following areas would it be most helpful for you to grow in your 360-degree leadership over the next month? The box you select will help you focus on the most impactful Skills in Action Activity for developing your interpersonal leadership right now.

❑ Improve your team's relationships by working through a 360-degree team-building exercise.
(Skills in Action: Develop 360-Degree Leadership As a Team, p. 70)

❑ Evaluate the strength of your current team's in Character, Competence, and Chemistry.
(Skills in Action: Evaluating Your Team, p. 72)

❑ Create interview questions to evaluate new future team members using Character, Competence, and Chemistry.
(Skills in Action: Develop an Interview Hiring Guide, p. 74)

❑ Break down lateral barriers and strengthen your peer relationships.
(Skills in Action: Build Influential Relationships with Your Peers, p. 75)

❑ Consider better ways to lead up.
(Skills in Action: Build an Authentic Relationship with Your Supervisor, p. 76)

10. My Skills in Action is: _____

o Share the activity you selected with your learning group.

SESSION WRAP-UP (5 minutes)

Close your time in prayer, asking God to help each member make measurable gains in 360-degree leadership over the next month.

> *Leadership is a relationally intensive activity. Developing your relational skills will help you move your initiatives from here to there. Read through the five Skills in Action for 360-degree leadership on the pages that follow and take action by doing at least one activity over the next month.*

SKILLS IN ACTION ACTIVITIES
SESSION 3: Mastering 360-Degree Leadership

As leaders move an initiative from here to there, they will inevitably interact with and need to influence other people. In addition to our relationships with the people who serve on our teams, all of us are also accountable to supervisors above us and laterally to colleagues who are working on different aspects of the overall mission.

The Interpersonal Leadership element of the *Leading from Here to There* framework covers all the various skills around the people side of leadership. Jesus tells his disciples that he expects them to lead by serving others, not lording it over and exercising authority (Matthew 20:25–28). Action-oriented and goal-focused leaders should not prioritize accomplishing tasks without giving adequate thought to how people are treated in the process. Building your ability to be an effective 360-degree leader may be one of the biggest challenges you face as a leader.

Most books on leadership address how to lead down with people who report to you. Less material is available to help you understand how to lead up and laterally. Despite the lack of available resources, the reality is that your effectiveness and success are dependent on each of these relationships. You must thoughtfully and intentionally lead with your supervisor(s) and peers, in addition to your direct reports. Your potential as a leader will be limited if you don't invest time and effort with each relationship.

Take action on your 360-degree leadership skills by implementing at least one of the Skills in Action activities.

SKILLS IN ACTION ACTIVITIES:
Mastering 360-Degree Leadership

Develop 360-Degree Leadership as a Team   PAGE 70

Discuss 360-degree leadership with your team and talk about how your team is doing when it comes to managing relationships.

Evaluating Your Team   PAGE 72

Use Character, Competence, and Chemistry to evaluate your team— and develop action steps for improvement.

Develop an Interview Guide   PAGE 74

Create an interview guide with your team using Character, Competence, and Chemistry to help you screen and interview future candidates and volunteers.

Build Influential Relationships with Your Peers   PAGE 75

Review your Relationship Map on page 63 and develop in-depth plans to serve, celebrate, and improve your peer relationships.

Build an Authentic Relationship with Your Supervisor   PAGE 76

Identify and confirm preferences for how you and your supervisor work together.

Visionary

Self

INTERPERSONAL

Organizational

Calling

SKILLS IN ACTION
Develop 360-Degree Leadership as a Team

Discussing 360-degree leadership with your team could be a highly engaging and educational experience and can go a long way toward building a fantastic team environment. Including your team in this activity will build a shared understanding of 360-degree leadership dynamics and can ultimately improve your team's effectiveness.

Gather your team together and introduce the concepts of 360-degree leadership using the video segment or your own summary of 360-degree leadership.

1. Post three flip charts in different corners of the room. Label one chart each as noted below.

2. Ask team members to split up evenly at each chart, discuss the questions on their chart, and record their answers.

3. When the groups are finished, ask someone from each group to present their charts to the whole group. Ask the group as a whole for their input and reactions as they listen to the presentations. Reinforce and summarize important points that the groups present. (Note: If your team is smaller, consider working through each chart together, as a team.)

SUPERVISOR(S)	PEERS	DIRECT REPORTS
What I need from her...	What I need from them...	What I need from them...
What she needs from me...	What they need from me...	What they need from me...
Tips for a strong relationship...	Tips for a strong relationship...	Tips for a strong relationship...

4. After your team has discussed all three charts, lead a discussion on how the team is doing as it relates to the 360-degree tips shared. Where is the team strong? Where can the team improve?

5. Close your time by asking the team to discuss what next steps they agree to take together.

This activity can take from one hour to 90 minutes, depending on the size of your team and the depth of your conversation.

 Once you have completed your activity, go to Now What? on page 78 for additional ideas, next steps, and resources.

SKILLS IN ACTION
Evaluating Your Team

Managing your team is more than just assigning tasks to people and assessing how they did. In addition to managing their work, Bill suggested using the C's to build and guide your team's development. With your current team in mind, answer the questions below.

Using the chart that follows, how would you rate your team in each of these areas? (Use extra paper if you need to add more people to your list.)

H = High (This team member is very strong in this area)	M = Medium (This team member exhibits strong points and weak points in this area.)	Low = Low (I have serious doubts or concerns about this team member in this area)	? = Unsure (I am unsure or need more information)

NAME	STRENGTH IN EACH "C" (HIGH, MEDIUM, LOW, OR UNSURE)			THE MOST CRITICAL "C"
	Character	Competence	Chemistry	

As you review each team member you rated, which "C" do you feel is most hindering their development as a leader or their contributions to your team? Write that "C" in the final column, under "The most critical C."

For the areas where you marked with a question mark (i.e., don't have enough information), how will you learn more or gather information to help you assess them?

Schedule a meeting with each direct report to discuss your evaluation. Be sure to celebrate the areas where you have evaluated him or her as "high." If there are any "low" points, the following action steps might be considered:

- **Character concerns:** discuss specific situations where you see character deficiencies and develop a plan with the team member to address those deficiencies.
- **Competency concerns:** clarify the area(s) of development needed and create a development plan with clear next steps.
- **Chemistry concerns:** sometimes supervisors can develop stronger chemistry with a team member by taking time getting to know the employee or volunteer better, both inside and outside of work. Schedule time to get to know the team member with whom you have low chemistry.

Keep your discussion focused on descriptive examples. It is not necessary to share the specific ratings—but instead focus on where to improve.

This activity can take one or more hours, depending on the size of your team and the number of conversations you have.

 Once you have completed your activity, go to Now What? on page 78 for additional ideas, next steps, and resources.

SKILLS IN ACTION
Develop an Interview Guide

Whether you are in the process of adding a new teammate or you plan to add one in the future, you can apply this session right away by developing an interview guide that will help you assess a candidate according to Character, Competence, and Chemistry. Discussing questions and strategies with your team will help you enter the hiring process with goals that are aligned.

Gather your team to brainstorm questions that will help you better assess potential new hires or team members. Assign someone to capture your ideas on a flip chart. Gather as many questions as you can.

- What kinds of interview questions or background information would help our team determine a candidate's character?

- How could we evaluate a candidate's competence? Their learning agility?

- What might help us determine if a potential teammate will have chemistry with our team?

Once you have listed out plenty of questions in each area, spend the last few minutes of your meeting determining the top three questions or strategies for each C. Have someone capture the team's consensus on the flip chart.

At the close of the meeting, assign someone to write or type up the questions in a document and distribute it to the team.

This activity can take from 45 to 90 minutes, depending on the size of your team and the depth of your conversation.

 Once you have completed your activity, go to Now What? on page 78 for additional ideas, next steps, and resources.

SKILLS IN ACTION
Build Influential Relationships with Your Peers

The development of strong peer relationships is a sign of healthy, high-functioning teams. When power struggles and competition increase among peers, not only does work suffer, but it harms relationships and damages your team's culture. You can improve your peer relationships by being more intentional in finding ways to support fellow team members.

Look back at your Relationship Map, found on page 63. Identify two or three peers with whom you would like to strengthen your relationship. Then identify what actions you can start and stop doing to improve these relationships.

Peer name	Start doing	Stop doing

Strengthening your peer relationships can take many months. To get started, schedule when you will implement one or two actions for each person over the next month. After each action, reflect and write some notes about what happened to your peer relationship as a result of what you started or stopped doing. How did this affect your peer? How did it affect your own heart toward that person? Be prepared to discuss your experience with your learning group.

This activity can take between 30 minutes and one hour for reflection and action plan.

 Once you have completed your activity, go to Now What? on page 78 for additional ideas, next steps, and resources.

Visionary

Self

INTERPERSONAL

Organizational

Calling

SKILLS IN ACTION
Build an Authentic Relationship with Your Supervisor

Every supervisor you ever have will have different expectations of you, a different leadership style, and different ways of working. You cannot take it for granted that you can work effectively in the same way with each one. It's important to take the time to get to know your current supervisor and identify the best ways to work with her.

You may find that your natural style works very easily with your supervisor's natural style. However, when this is not the case you can try to improve your relationship by seeking to influence a change with your supervisor or by adapting your ways of working to enhance your relationship.

Consider the three relational dynamics in the left column of the chart on page 77.

1. Write down how you prefer to work with your supervisor in each dynamic and what you think your supervisor's preferences may be.

2. Schedule a meeting with your supervisor to discuss your thoughts and ask for input on how you can enhance your working relationship.

3. After your meeting, take time to reflect on your discussion and make note of specific actions or behaviors you need to put in place to improve your relationship.

Note: It may feel risky to have a conversation like this with your supervisor. If you want to start this topic less directly, consider asking your supervisor alternative questions, such as:
- What are one or two ways we are working well together?
- What are one or two ways we could enhance how we work together?

Relationship dynamic	My preferences	Supervisor's preferences
COMMUNICATION Keeping your supervisor informed and vice versa; frequency and method of communication desired.		
DECISION MAKING Understanding when or how your supervisor wants to approve or veto decisions.		
INFLUENCE Giving your supervisor honest feedback regarding direction of efforts, decisions being made, or team dynamics.		
CONFLICT Knowing your supervisor's preferences for how and when to bring up disagreements.		

This activity can take between one and two hours, depending amount of preparation you do and the length of your time with your supervisor.

Once you have completed your activity, go to What? on page 78 for additional ideas, next steps, and resources.

NOW WHAT?

As the scope and scale of your leadership increases over time, the relational skills and associated dynamics get more complicated. The number of people, departments, roles, functions, and committees you must deal with increases and your leadership will be stretched in ways you didn't know were possible. You may find yourself involved in a lengthy process to gain agreement on tasks that seems straightforward and clear to you. People bring complexity to the process of aligning goals, negotiating priorities, approving funding, making decisions, and influencing change. Success is often determined by relational intelligence more than by intellect.

Along the way, you will consciously or unconsciously make choices about the kind of leader you will be. Become a student of the people around you, and seek to understand what each individual needs or wants—and why. Having a constant eye on the dynamics of your 360-degree relationships is often the first step toward proactive interpersonal leadership.

> HAVING A CONSTANT **EYE ON THE DYNAMICS** OF YOUR **360-DEGREE RELATIONSHIPS** IS OFTEN THE FIRST STEP TOWARD PROACTIVE **INTERPERSONAL LEADERSHIP.**

Revisit the Relationship Map regularly to assess the current status of your work or ministry relationships. Make it a priority to strengthen existing relationships and to build new ones. The time you spend building relational capital is never wasted. As you strengthen your relationships, you become a credible and trusted leader and will experience rewards by achieving excellent results. And even more importantly, you treasure that which God treasures most—people.

My Action Plan – Mastering 360-Degree Leadership

Use the chart below to plan your next step(s) in 360-degree leadership. Do you need to evaluate your team's Character, Competence, and Chemistry? Or maybe you need to work on your lateral relationships? Or improve your working relationship with your supervisor? Write your next step(s) in the chart below—thinking through a realistic deadline and other people you will need to include in your plan.

Next Step	By When	Who should I include?	Who could help or coach me?

BUILDING A FANTASTIC CULTURE

"Every culture can improve. And when a culture gets healthier and healthier, you can feel it in the hallways. You can feel it in the meetings. You can feel it in the parking lot. **And when people love their jobs, they outperform average workers by significant margins**, because they're giving their hearts and souls to the cause your organization represents."

—BILL HYBELS

LEARNING GROUP GATHERING

GROUP CHECK-IN (15 minutes)

Welcome to Session 4 of *Leading From Here to There*. A key part of learning any new skill is getting input from fellow learners. Before watching the video, debrief your Skills in Action from Session 3 on 360-Degree Leadership. Use the following questions to guide your discussion.

- Which Skills in Action Activity did you complete?
- How might your work or ministry interactions with others change as a result of the activity?
- What is the next step for you to grow in your 360-degree relationships?

VIDEO NOTES: Building a Fantastic Culture (25 minutes)

Play the video segment for Session 4. As you watch, use the outline below to follow along or to take notes.

NOTES

Culture: the way people behave and relate to each other

SESSION

4

Visionary · Self · Interpersonal · Organizational · Calling

SUGGESTED TIME:
90 minutes

Group Check-In:
15 minutes

Video:
25 minutes

Group Discussion:
40 minutes

My Leadership Challenge:
5 minutes

Session Wrap-Up:
5 minutes

Every conversation is either a culture builder or a culture buster.

Culture surveys

Note: Culture surveys by outside firms can be extremely helpful for larger organizations. However, it is possible to assess culture and engagement on a smaller scale using online surveys or other tools. (See Conduct a Culture Assessment, p. 95)

To improve your culture, you need to measure it.

○ Your culture will only be as healthy as the senior leader wants it to be

○ Fit concerns

DATA GIVES YOU
THE COURAGE
TO HAVE
CONVERSATIONS.

Enforcing culture

- Call fouls

- Catch people doing something right.

You can make any culture better.

GROUP DISCUSSION (40 minutes)

> **DEFINING TERMS**
>
> Among organizational leadership experts, the concepts of culture and employee engagement are closely intertwined. Workers who fit the culture of a team are typically more engaged. Most surveys, like the one Bill describes, measure engagement as well as staff culture.
>
> **Culture** is the character and personality of your team. It's what makes your team unique and is the sum of its values, behaviors, traditions, beliefs, interactions, and history together.
>
> **Engagement** is the emotional commitment the worker has to the team and its goals. When workers are emotionally committed, they actually care about their organization and have an internal drive to see their team succeed.

1. The apostle Paul described the kind of culture he wanted for the early church in this way: *"Get rid of all bitterness, rage and anger, brawling and slander, along with every form of malice. Be kind and compassionate to one another, forgiving each other, just as Christ God forgave you"* (Ephesians 4:31–32). How do Paul's instructions here align with the way Bill talked about culture in this session?

2. Bill said, "Your culture will only be as strong as the senior leader wants it to be." Think back on different jobs or ministry experiences you have had. How have you seen this principle play itself out?

3. How would you describe your culture to someone who is not familiar with your team?

4. Bill said culture is about behaviors. Behaviors flow out of values. Take a few minutes on your own to evaluate your team's current practices on culture using the following scales.

1 _____ 2 _____ 3 _____ 4 _____ 5

Our cultural values are
not defined clearly.

Our cultural values
are clearly defined.

1 _____ 2 _____ 3 _____ 4 _____ 5

To my knowledge, we
have never measured
our culture.

We regularly measure
our culture.

1 _____ 2 _____ 3 _____ 4 _____ 5

We don't regularly
identify or celebrate
our culture builders.

We regularly identify
and celebrate our
culture builders.

1 _____ 2 _____ 3 _____ 4 _____ 5

People who violate our
culture usually are not
held accountable.

We call fouls
when there is a
culture violation.

1 _____ 2 _____ 3 _____ 4 _____ 5

We don't have good
ways to identify future
team members who fit
our culture.

We identify people who fit
our culture when adding
new team members.

When you are done, and to the degree you are comfortable, share your assessments with your learning group.

o What are the cultural strengths of your organization?

o Which areas might be improved?

5. Describe the characteristics of a person on your team who embodies your team's cultural values.

6. How does your team handle culture-buster behavior? Share best practices with your learning group.

7. If you need to call fouls over a long enough period of time, a teammate may become a "fit concern" (to use Bill's term). A fit concern refers to team members who are not a fit for their roles due to cultural mismatches or unmet performance expectations. Bill described his approach to handing these situations.

   - What did you think about his fit concern time frames?

   - How does your team handle fit concerns?

MY LEADERSHIP CHALLENGE (5 minutes)

As you close your learning group time, take the last 5 minutes to consider your personal takeaway(s) and select the Skills in Action activities that you will work on from this session.

8. My top one or two personal takeaway(s) are:

1	

2	

9. Consider the level of clarity your team currently has concerning culture. Which of the following practices could help improve your culture?

❑ Identify and define my team's top five values and culture.
   (Skills in Action: Identify your Team's Culture/Values Card Sort, p. 92)

❑ Make a plan and measure my team's culture.
   (Skills in Action: Conduct a Culture Assessment, p. 95)

❑ Create interview questions to assess future team members for cultural fit.
   (Skills in Action: Create an Interview Guide for Culture, p. 98)

❑ Become intentional in identifying culture builders and culture busters.
   (Skills in Action: Identify Your Culture Builders and Busters, p. 99)

❑ Evaluate the alignment of my personal cultural preferences with the culture of my current team.
   (Skills in Action: Assess the Best Culture Fit for You, p. 101)

10. My Skills in Action is: _____

   o Share the activity you selected with your learning group.

SESSION WRAP-UP (5 minutes)

Close your time in prayer, asking God to help each member do the hard work of improving their team's culture over the next month.

Now that you have identified the culture-building activity that will most impact your leadership, use the following pages to take action with your team. Read through the five Skills in Action activities for culture-building on the pages that follow, and make a plan right now to accomplish at least one activity over the next month.

SKILLS IN ACTION ACTIVITIES
SESSION 4: Building a Fantastic Culture

Culture is the way people on a team relate and behave toward each other on the way to mission achievement. It is formed out of values. Unless leaders take care to uphold and enforce a preferred culture, teams might achieve their *here* to *there* vision—but they will likely sustain some relational wounds along the way.

Leaders can't assume culture will take care of itself. A thriving culture takes intentionality on the leader's part. In his letter to the believers in Ephesus, the apostle Paul focused on right values and behaviors as he sought to develop a culture of grace and kindness in the early church. He wrote, *"Get rid of all bitterness, rage and anger, brawling and slander, along with every form of malice. Be kind and compassionate to one another, forgiving each other, just as in Christ God forgave you"* (Ephesians 4:31–32).

If you want to understand and improve your team's culture, you must engage in a process to understand it, measure it, and enforce it. The first step is to identify shared values and behaviors. This can be an exhilarating and clarifying process for teams to engage in together.

Once a team gains clarity on its shared values, it's time to measure how well your team is doing at matching those values to its behaviors. Data collection can be done by an outside firm—or it also can be done on a smaller scale with short internal surveys.

After values are measured, leaders enforce culture by finding opportunities to talk about it: sharing the results of culture surveys, celebrating culture builders, and calling fouls against culture busters. Team cultures flourish when all team members engage in enforcing and living the values.

Consider the current culture of your team or organization and what it might take to improve its health. Choose a Skills in Action Activity and start making progress toward a flourishing culture!

SKILLS IN ACTION ACTIVITIES:
Building a Fantastic Culture

If you are just starting to understand your team's culture, try this order:

1. Identify Your Team's Culture (Values Card Sort)

2. Conduct a Culture Assessment

The other activities refer back to these activities and flow out of them, based on the needs of your team.

Identify Your Team's Culture (Values Card Sort) PAGE 92

If your team does not yet have clearly identified cultural values, use this activity to identify and agree on the top five values for your team.

Conduct a Culture Assessment PAGE 95

If you have clearly identified values, this exercise allows you to measure the engagement and culture of your team.

Create an Interview Guide for Culture PAGE 98

Use this approach to involve your team in creating an interview guide to screen and interview candidates to ensure a strong cultural fit.

Identify Your Culture Builders and Culture Busters PAGE 99

Reinforce your cultural values by using this process for recognizing cultural builders and for calling fouls when needed.

Assess the Best Culture Fit for You PAGE 101

This self-evaluative exercise will help you identify the attributes of the type of culture in which your leadership can best thrive.

SKILLS IN ACTION
Identify Your Team's Culture (Values Card Sort)

If your team has not defined common core values, this activity gives you an opportunity to identify values that will lay the cultural foundation for your team. Schedule a team discussion focusing on these values.

Before the meeting, make a set of values cards for each team member using the list of values on the next two pages. The list includes common values that a team might have. Feel free to add values on the blank cards that you think will be important to your team. Each team member will need one full set of cards.

- Distribute the values cards to each team member. Ask them to rank their top five values on a flip chart or white board and share why they chose them. Allowing team members time to talk about what is important to them is a critical step in this activity. Then, lead your team in discussing how you might narrow down the possible choices.

- Once they have discussed their values, ask team members to determine the top five.

- It is okay to include an aspirational value on your list—a value that may not currently be part of your team culture but where your team wants to grow.

- Close with a discussion on what actions the team can take to live out these values day-to-day.

This activity can take between one and two hours, depending on the size of your team and the depth of your conversation.

 Once you have completed your activity, go to Now What? on page 104 for additional ideas, next steps, and resources.

ACHIEVEMENT Successfully complete tangible tasks or projects	**AESTHETIC** Share a desire for beauty; value musical and artistic expression	**AUTHORITY** Have the power to direct events and make things happen
COMMUNITY Live in fellowship with others both inside and outside of work	**COMPETENCE** Be good at what we do; exhibit skills needed to accomplish goals	**CONSENSUS** Make decisions everyone can live with
COURAGE Stand up for beliefs; overcome fear; challenge conventional wisdoms	**DIPLOMACY** Find common ground with difficult people and situations, resolving conflict; communicate with tact	**EMPOWERMENT** Give team members the responsibility, authority, resources and support to make decisions and take actions in their areas
FORGIVENESS Willingly pardon others and let go of hurt	**HELPING** Take care of others; do what teammates need	**INNOVATION** Transform new technologies into new products; value and reward creativity
INTEGRITY Display honesty, openness, fairness, high professional standards; keep promises; uphold ethical and legal conduct	**INTIMACY** Show deep emotional, spiritual connection	**KNOWLEDGE** Seek intellectual stimulation, new ideas, truth, and understanding

Visionary

Self

Interpersonal

ORGANIZATIONAL

Calling

PERSEVERANCE Push through to the end, completing tasks	**PERSONAL GROWTH** Engage in continual learning, development of new skill, and increased self-awareness	**PLAY** Be open to fun, lightheartedness, and spontaneity
QUALITY Understand and exceed the requirements of customers	**RATIONALITY** Display consistent, logical, clear reasoning; keep emotions in check	**RESPECT FOR INDIVIDUALS** Treat others with dignity and respect; share information; listen well; value everyone's unique contributions
STABILITY Display certainty and predictability	**TEAMWORK** Work openly and supportively with others toward a common goal; take pride in joint accomplishments	

The Values Card Sort Activity is based on Scott, Jaffe, and Tobe's book, *Organizational Vision, Values, and Mission*, Crisp Publications, 1992.

SKILLS IN ACTION
Conduct a Culture Assessment

Assess the engagement and culture of your team by creating and distributing a survey using the sample engagement questions and rating scale provided on the next page. Communicate the purpose of the survey to your team in advance. If your team has identifiable cultural values, be sure to include specific questions to measure them in survey questions 9–13. Delete these questions if your team doesn't have stated values. (If you haven't identified values for your team, either delete questions 9–13 from your survey or consider doing Skills in Action: Identify Your Team's Culture/Values Card Sort.)

You can distribute and tally your survey on paper and by hand, but free online programs like SurveyMonkey, Google Forms, and others make the distribution, tallying, analyzing, and reporting of your assessment easier and more professional.

Distribute the survey. Let your team know that the survey is confidential and encourage them to be completely honest in their responses. To maintain confidentiality, choose a neutral person (someone from outside your team) to collect and tally the surveys or develop the online reports once your data has been gathered. Give participants a deadline that allows them to complete the survey in an unrushed manner—from several days up to two weeks. Send a reminder the day before your deadline to help ensure you get 100% participation.

After everyone has taken the survey and your neutral helper has compiled your results, gather your team to discuss the questions below.

- What are the trends or commonalities in the feedback?

- What observations do you have about the things we are doing well?

- What observations do you have about the things we can do better? (Ask for specific examples to help clarify improvement opportunities.)

- What actions can we take to improve our team culture? What should we stop doing? What should we start doing? What should we continue doing?

- Who is responsible for accomplishing our Action Step? By when?

ENGAGEMENT SURVEY

		STRONGLY DISAGREE	DISAGREE	NEITHER DISAGREE NOR AGREE	AGREE	STRONGLY AGREE
1	I am really enthusiastic about the mission of my company.					
2	At work, I clearly understand what's expected of me.					
3	On my team, I am surrounded by people who share my values.					
4	I have the chance to use my strengths every day at work.					
5	My teammates have my back.					
6	I know I will be recognized for excellent work.					
7	I have great confidence in my company's future.					
8	In my work I am always challenged to grow.					

Questions 1-8 on this Engagement Survey were developed by The Marcus Buckingham Company in conjunction with SurveyMonkey. This package, called the StandOut Engagement Pulse Survey, can be found at www.surveymonkey.com/mp/team-standout-engagement-pulse-survey/.

		STRONGLY DISAGREE	DISAGREE	NEITHER DISAGREE NOR AGREE	AGREE	STRONGLY AGREE
9	In my team, we live out our value of _____.					
10	In my team, we live out our value of _____.					
11	In my team, we live out our value of _____.					
12	In my team, we live out our value of _____.					
13	In my team, we live out our value of _____.					

NOTE: This simple survey works well for small organizations or teams. If you would like to measure culture in a larger organization, you might consider hiring an outside firm. One that Bill Hybels recommends is Best Christian Workplace Institute. (www.bcwinstitute.com)

This activity can take between one and two hours, depending on the size of your team and your method of survey distribution.

 Once you have completed your activity, go to Now What? on page 104 for additional ideas, next steps, and resources.

SKILLS IN ACTION
Create an Interview Guide for Culture

This activity will give your team the opportunity to develop interview questions that will guide the selection or hiring of future team members. Involving your team in creating a guide will help you screen candidates who will be good cultural fits and to assess their skills and values more efficiently.

Ask team members, individually or in pairs, to develop six to eight interview questions that get at the heart of each of your stated values. (See Identify Your Team's Culture/Values Card Sort Activity on page 92.) Meet as a team to share questions and select the best ones to establish the interview guide.

Once you have selected the best questions, discuss how you will use the interview guide as a team and consider practicing on one another to see how well the questions work. Make adjustments as needed, and then commit to using your new guide. Select one team member to write the questions down and to deliver them to each team member for future use.

This activity can take from 30 minutes to one hour, depending on the size of your team and the depth of your conversation.

 Once you have completed your activity, go to Now What? on page 104 for additional ideas, next steps, and resources.

SKILLS IN ACTION
Identify Your Culture Builders and Culture Busters

Every action you take on your team is either a culture builder or a culture buster. You reinforce cultural values by giving recognition to culture builders and calling fouls when someone isn't living up to the stated values. By so doing, you protect the culture you are trying to build.

Plan to take time during your next team meeting to talk about culture builders and busters.

Prepare for the meeting by engaging in some self-reflection:

- Revisit your cultural values. (See Identify Your Team's Culture/Values Card Sort Activity on page 92.) Are there two or three people who really live out one of your cultural values? Identify specific examples. Think of a tangible way you can honor them in front of their peers.

- Honestly assess where culture busting exists, including areas where you might be falling short. Identify toxic behaviors that may be creeping in. Think of appropriate ways to address those behaviors during your meeting without dishonoring anyone, and encourage your group to do better.

During the meeting:

- Label two flip charts

CULTURE BUILDERS	CULTURE BUSTERS

- Pass out your team's stated cultural values and discuss how culture flows out of values and behaviors.

- Have one person act as the scribe—and fill out the charts with culture building actions and culture busting actions.

- Since it is sometimes hard to discuss culture busting, to increase comfort, have teammates break into groups of two or three. Be prepared to "break the ice" by going first—possibly admitting times you busted the culture or when you observed it happening.

- If it is possible, identify some people who consistently build the culture and tangibly honor them in front of their peers.

- Close your meeting by having team members share ways they can revisit this topic on an ongoing basis.

NOTE: If there is a specific person you need to confront about culture busting, do not do so in front of the group. Rather, schedule a one-on-one meeting to discuss how their behavior is negatively impacting your team's culture.

This activity can take from one hour to 90 minutes, depending on the size of your team and the depth of your conversation.

 Once you have completed your activity, go to Now What? on page 104 for additional ideas, next steps, and resources.

SKILLS IN ACTION
Assess the Best Culture Fit for You

Sometimes, you will find yourself working in an environment that simply does not fit your values or style. Perhaps your team values a fast pace and quick decision making, but you are more deliberative in nature and prefer to take the time necessary to make the best decisions. Or perhaps your team values staying the course and doing things that are tried and true, but you value change and are energized by trying new things and looking for better solutions.

Reflect on the attributes of an ideal culture in which you would thrive. Having clarity on what is important to you helps you determine the right culture for you—whether you are a cultural misfit with your current team, if there is room for you to try to influence your team's culture so there is greater alignment, or if there is no margin for adjustment and the misalignment is too great.

Schedule time with a peer, mentor, or supervisor to discuss your thoughts about the ideal cultural fit for you at work. Prepare for that meeting by reflecting on and writing out your answers to the questions below. Develop a list of characteristics for your ideal work culture. When you discuss your thoughts with your friend/mentor/supervisor, ask for their help and encouragement about the right next steps for you.

- What attributes in a supervisor are important to you and why?

- How important is formal structure to you? Structure may include clarity in reporting relationships, processes and procedures, role definition, or policies.

- Using the cards from Skills in Action Activity: Identify Your Team's Culture, identify the top five values you seek in a team culture.

You:	Your Team:
1.	1.
2.	2.
3.	3.
4.	4.
5.	5.

- Based on your answers above, how aligned are your personal cultural preferences with the culture in which you currently work?

- How might you need to adapt to the culture of your team? Can you lean into commonalities and still thrive?

- How might you positively influence your team's culture?

- If you cannot influence or adapt, what next steps might you need to take?

This activity can take between one hour and two hours, depending on the depth of your reflections and the length of your meeting.

 Once you have completed your activity, go to Now What? on page 104 for additional ideas, next steps, and resources.

NOW WHAT?

Early in his ministry, Bill naively thought culture would take care of itself. But he learned that creating and maintaining a thriving culture takes intentionality. Even after you have done the work to identify and measure your culture, you need to engage in the ongoing work of enforcing your culture. Data gives you the confidence to have conversations that you should have been having all along. If every person on your team understands and is working to build your culture, it will get better!

In addition to the people side of culture, there are some less obvious expressions of your culture, as well. Processes, procedures, policies, the way you handle meetings, and your communication practices are all reflections of your culture. They send a message about what is important to your team. For example, if you listed "innovation" as a value, but leadership consistently rewards safe behavior, teammates might call foul. Team members are quick to spot inconsistency when stated values and actual behaviors don't align.

> THE DATA GIVES YOU THE
> **CONFIDENCE**
> TO HAVE CONVERSATIONS
> THAT YOU SHOULD HAVE BEEN
> HAVING ALL ALONG.

After you've identified culture builders and busters from a people perspective, take time to assess these less obvious indicators of your culture. Consider assigning a team member to evaluate your processes to be sure they are congruent with your identified cultural values. Do your processes support or get in the way of your preferred culture? As you include your team members in the process of identifying areas of misalignment, they will begin to take ownership. And once everyone is an owner, you are well on your way to building a culture that thrives.

My Action Plan – Building a Fantastic Culture

Use the chart below to plan your next steps in Culture. Do you need to identify your values or measure your team's engagement? Is there a tough conversation you need to have with a teammate to "call a foul"? Or maybe you see processes or procedures that are antithetical to the culture you want to build. Write your next step(s) in the chart below—thinking through a realistic deadline and other people you will need to include in your plan.

Next Step	By When	Who should I include?	Who could help or coach me?

PURSUE YOUR UNIQUE CALLING

Most of us duck visions that feel
scary or we don't take them as far
as they could go because we feel inadequate.
Somehow we've got to get over this stuff.
**Leaders have got to step into the vision
God wants them to lead** and face
their fears down—and get on with it.
We'd have a better world.

—BILL HYBELS

LEARNING GROUP GATHERING

GROUP CHECK-IN (15 minutes)

Welcome to Session 5 of *Leading from Here to There*. A key part of learning any new skill is getting input from fellow learners. Before watching the video, debrief your Skills in Action Activity from Session 4: Building a Fantastic Culture.

- Which Skills in Action Activity did you complete?
- What have you learned about your team's culture?
- If you did an exercise with your team, how did they respond?
- What are some next steps for your team in building a fantastic culture?

VIDEO NOTES: Pursue Your Unique Calling
(20 minutes)

Play the video segment for Session 5. As you watch, use the outline below to follow along or to take notes.

NOTES

SUGGESTED TIME:
90 minutes

Group Check-In:
15 minutes

Video:
20 minutes

Group Discussion:
45 minutes

My Leadership Challenge:
5 minutes

Session Wrap-Up:
5 minutes

GOD... CALLED US WITH A
HOLY CALLING,
NOT ACCORDING TO OUR WORKS, BUT ACCORDING TO HIS OWN
PURPOSE AND GRACE.

2 TIMOTHY 1:9 (NKJV)

The idea of calling is central to leadership.

God has given you aptitudes, spiritual gifts, and passion.

"Top box" and "white-hot why"

Calling unfolds over time, through trial and error.

Fear

> WALK IN THE GENERAL
> DIRECTION YOU THINK
> **GOD WANTS YOU**
> TO GO AND MAKE
> COURSE ADJUSTMENTS.

Sometimes, callings are fueled by positive vision.

Other times, callings are fueled by negative energy.

> FOR WE ARE HIS HANDIWORK,
> CREATED IN CHRIST JESUS TO DO
> **GOOD WORKS,**
> WHICH GOD PREPARED IN
> ADVANCE FOR US TO DO.
>
> EPHESIANS 2:10

Leadership matters.

GROUP DISCUSSION (40 minutes)

1. Ephesians 2:10 says, *"For we are his handiwork, created in Christ Jesus to do good works, which God prepared in advance for us to do."* With this verse in mind, share your initial reactions to Bill's thoughts on calling in the video.

2. Do you think that God has a specific and unique calling for every person? Why or why not?

3. Do you have a sense about what your calling might be? If yes, in what ways are you living out your calling now?

4. Bill said calling unfolds over time through trial and error and that we should maintain the mindset to be always leadable by God. How do you feel about the idea that your calling may shift or change over time? How can you ensure that you stay open and leadable over time?

5. Bill said that God has given all of us aptitudes (skills), spiritual gifts, and passions. One way to get insight into your passion is to pay attention to issues that you care about. Passion is often related to specific social issues or people groups. Using the list below, circle the top two or three items from each list that grab your attention.

People Groups:

Abused	Formerly incarcerated	Orphans/foster kids	Junior high students
Artists	Fathers/men	Parents of teens	High school students
Business leaders	Homeless	Poor	College students
Children	Hospitalized	Incarcerated	Special needs
Disabled	Internationals	Refugees	Teen moms
Divorced people	Immigrants	Sex workers	Dying
LGBT	Single parents	War/crime victims	Elderly
Mentally ill	Babies and preschool	Moms/women	Empty nesters
Millennials	Elementary students	Young married	ESL speakers
New parents	Unemployed	Other:	

Social Issues:

Abortion	Evangelism	Job creation	Politics
Addiction	Family	Justice	Poverty
AIDS	Gambling	Literacy	Racism
Bullying	Gender issues	Loneliness	Spiritual emptiness
Childcare	Grief or loss	Marriage/divorce	Suicide
Church planting	Healthcare	Mental health	Technology
Depression	Human trafficking	Nutrition	Terrorism
Economic empowerment	Hunger	Environment	Violence/gangs
Education	Immigration	Foster care/adoption	War
Income inequality	Other:		

How could you apply your skills and spiritual gifts to these passion areas? Write your thoughts below, then share your insights with your learning group.

6. Sometimes we get clues about our calling when God inspires us with a positive vision. At other times, we feel our calling most deeply when we experience frustration (a "holy discontent") about an issue that just is not right in this world. Take a few minutes to fill out the columns below. Then share with your learning group.

Times I felt inspired by a positive vision	Times I was exposed to a situation that "wrecked" me

7. When you think about your current leadership role—paid or unpaid—which phrase best describes your alignment with your calling? If you feel comfortable, share your thoughts with your learning group.

❑ I am leading within my calling right now.

❑ I am leading near my calling, but I need to shift a few things to be more fully aligned.

❑ I sense I might need to stop what I am currently doing in order to pursue my calling.

❑ I am not sure of my calling right now, but I am walking in the direction God is leading, trusting him to guide me.

❑ Other _____

8. Sometimes, we can let fear stand in the way of pursuing our callings. The following are common fears that can become barriers.

- Safety/Security
- Ability/Confidence
- Approval/Acceptance

Discuss with your learning group. Which of these fears, if any, tends to hold you back from fully pursuing your calling?

What might help you overcome that fear or barrier?

MY LEADERSHIP CHALLENGE (5 minutes)

As you close your learning group time, take the last 5 minutes to consider your personal takeaway(s) and identify which Skills in Action Activity would be most helpful for you to focus on from this session.

9. My top two personal takeaways are:

1

2

10. Which of the following areas would be most helpful for you to grow in your calling over the next month? The box you select will help you focus on the most impactful Skills In Action Activity for your leadership right now.

  ❏ I need to take steps to understand myself better and to identify my calling.
  (Skills in Action: Identify Your Calling, p. 118)

  ❏ I have a sense about my calling, but it would be helpful to do more exploration to confirm this direction.
  (Skills in Action: Explore Your Calling, p. 120)

  ❏ I need to evaluate my current work or ministry assignment for its alignment with my calling.
  (Skills in Action: Evaluate the Alignment of Your Calling, p. 122)

  ❏ I need to identify the fears that are holding me back and develop steps to overcome them.
  (Skills in Action: Identify and Overcome Your Fears, p. 124)

11. My Skills in Action is: _____

  ○ Share the activity you selected with your learning group.

12. Schedule a one-hour Time to Celebrate gathering with your learning group at the end of the coming month. You can also debrief your Skills in Action activities from this session.

SESSION WRAP-UP (5 minutes)
Close your time in prayer, thanking God for how he has grown your group through this study, and asking him to help each member understand their calling.

> *Now that you have identified the activity that will most help you identify and live out your calling, read through the Skills in Action activities on the pages that follow, and make a plan to accomplish at least one activity over the next month.*

God has called you to be a leader—and he wants you to engage your leadership to accomplish his vital work in this world. Leaders who have a deep understanding of the work God is calling them to do in the world—and then endeavor to move that work "from here to there"—enter into the grand adventure God has planned for their lives!

All other elements of the *Leading from Here to There* framework address the "hows" of leadership. The Calling element identifies the "where" or the "why." The apostle Paul, in his letter to believers in Ephesus, writes, *"We are God's handiwork, created in Christ Jesus to do good works, which God prepared in advance for us to do"* (Ephesians 2:10). The focus of your leadership energy is directed to a specific issue, process, or cause God has prepared in advance for you.

Sometimes our callings lines up nicely with our jobs. At other times, for a variety of reasons, pay and passion do not add up to meet both our financial and job satisfaction needs. Do not feel discouraged if this applies to you. You can answer your calling in your home, as a volunteer, or in a part-time capacity. Whether you pursue your calling vocationally or as a volunteer, your leadership makes a difference!

Step into your calling and be the best leader you can be in every area you lead. Complete one or more of the following Skills in Action activities to help you explore, identify, and evaluate your calling.

SKILLS IN ACTION ACTIVITIES:
Pursue Your Unique Calling

Identify Your Calling   PAGE 118

If you are just beginning to consider your calling, or if you are sensing God might be leading you to make a shift, these activities help you identify new arenas in which to exercise your leadership.

Explore Your Calling   PAGE 120

Use this approach if you have a good sense about your calling but want to go deeper to confirm your direction.

Evaluate the Alignment of Your Calling   PAGE 122

These exercises are designed to help you evaluate the alignment of your calling to your current life situation, work or ministry role.

Identify and Overcome Your Fear   PAGE 124

If fear is holding you back from pursuing your calling, this activity will help you identify what is driving the fear and show ways to overcome the fear.

Visionary

Self

Interpersonal

Organizational

CALLING

SKILLS IN ACTION
Identify Your Calling

If you are just beginning to identify your calling or you sense that God might be leading you to make a shift, schedule a time to meet with a friend or mentor to discuss what your calling might be and how to discern what God may be telling you.

1) Complete at least one of the mini-activities below.

2) Reflect on the results of these activities and write out the insights you gained.

3) Meet with a friend or mentor to discuss your insights and impressions.

MINI-ACTIVITIES

Personal Assessment

Bill said that your calling is aligned with the aptitudes (skills or strengths), spiritual gifts, and passions God has given you. Reflect on and write about the following questions:

- What practical skills do you possess? In what fields are you trained? (i.e., accounting, medicine, carpentry)

- What are you good at? List out your top three to five strengths. If you want help defining your strengths, take the assessment found in *StrengthsFinder 2.0* by Tom Rath.

- What are your spiritual gifts? If you want help defining your spiritual gifts, take the assessment found in *Network* by Bruce Bugbee.

- Do you have a clear idea about your passions? Look back at the issues you identified on page 112 and write out your insights.

Look Back at Trends in Your Life

Draw a "life line" that charts your life's highs and lows. Journal about the highs and lows and any patterns you see, identifying the events and experiences that shaped you. How might the story of your life to date give you hints about your calling?

Scan the News

When you read news stories online or in the newspaper, what issues stand out to you? Which topics or events make your pulse quicken? Which incite strong emotional reactions—anger, frustration, or joy? How might your interest in these events relate to your calling?

REFLECTION QUESTIONS

- What have you learned about your calling?

- Take a few minutes to pray that God will speak into your reflections. What might he be saying to you about your calling?

- What questions about your calling could you process with a friend or mentor? Write down the questions you would like to ask.

This activity can take between 90 minutes and three hours, depending on the depth of your reflection and the length of your meeting time with your friend or mentor.

 Once you have completed your activity, go to Now What? on page 134 for additional ideas, next steps, and resources.

SKILLS IN ACTION
Explore Your Calling

Sometimes, we think we know what our calling might be, but additional exploration might help to confirm our direction.

1) Complete one or more of the mini-activities below.

2) Reflect on the results of these activities and journal about the insights you have gained.

3) Meet with a friend or mentor to discuss your calling and how you can confirm what God may be telling you.

MINI-ACTIVITIES

Take a Field Trip
Go on a firsthand expedition to experience something that grabs your attention. What effect did the experience have on you?

Meet with Someone
Arrange to meet with someone in a field related to your calling to learn more. Journal about the insights you gained.

Read a Book/Watch a TED Talk
Read one or more books on the subjects that grab your attention—or watch a TED Talk or similar video. Did your interest expand? Do you have more questions? Can you picture yourself getting involved? Journal about your insights.

Watch a Movie
Explore others' life stories through movies or documentaries on subjects that relate to your thoughts about calling. Is your interest expanding or shrinking? Journal about the insights you gained.

REFLECTION QUESTIONS

- What have you learned about your calling?

- Take a few minutes to pray that God will speak into your reflections. What might he be saying to you about your calling?

- What questions about your calling could you process with a friend or mentor? Write down the questions you would like to ask.

This activity can take from one hour to a full day, depending on the activity you select and the length of your meeting with your friend or mentor.

 Once you have completed your activity, go to Now What? on page 134 for additional ideas, next steps, and resources.

SKILLS IN ACTION
Evaluate the Alignment of Your Calling

If you are currently in a role that seems somewhat close to your calling, evaluate the level of alignment through this activity.

1) Complete the activities below.

2) Reflect on the results and write out the insights you gained.

3) Meet with a friend or mentor to discuss your evaluation and share ideas on what your next steps might be.

ASSESS YOUR ALIGNMENT

Evaluate your current job, ministry role, and personal life by listing areas of alignment and misalignment below:

Aspects of my life that align with my calling	Aspects of my life that DON'T align with my calling

What are some ways you can bring your life into better alignment with your calling?

- How would you break down the steps necessary to create better alignment?

- Do you need more education or different experiences to better align your calling?

- Can alignment be achieved in your current role and organization, or would you need to make a shift?

EVALUATE YOUR CALENDAR

How we spend our time is a window into whether our lives are aligned with our calling. Look at the activities that have filled your calendar at work and at home over the past month. How many activities are aligned with your calling? Journal about how you might better align your calendar with your calling.

REFLECTION QUESTIONS

- What degree of alignment exists between your current life situation and your calling?

- What could you change to bring about greater alignment?

- What would be the implications of such a change? (Consider various aspects of your life such as family, vocation, education, pay, and living arrangements.)

- What questions about your calling evaluation could you process with a friend or mentor? Write down the questions you would like to ask.

This activity can take between 90 minutes and three hours, depending on the depth of your reflection and the length of your meeting time with your friend or mentor.

 Once you have completed your activity, go to Now What? on page 134 for additional ideas, next steps, and resources.

SKILLS IN ACTION
Identify and Overcome Your Fear

In the video, Bill said that fear is often the biggest reason many people don't live out their callings. If you resonated with Bill's words or felt a conviction from God during that part of the session, perhaps you have heard God's whisper toward a particular cause or situation, but have not yet followed up on that leading due—at least in part—to a particular fear you need to confront.

You're in good company. God's trademark pattern throughout the pages of Scripture is to call people for tasks that feel bigger than they can handle—and with that comes fear. Consider Moses. In Exodus chapters 3 and 4, Moses receives huge marching orders from God: to lead the Israelites out of their bondage in Egypt to the Promised Land. Look at the list of excuses Moses gives God as to why he is not the right guy for the job:

- Who am I to do this? (Exodus 3:11)

- What if they don't believe this is from God? (Exodus 3:13)

- What if I don't have the right skills for the job? (Exodus 4:10)

- Please send someone else! (Exodus 4:13)

God lovingly and graciously takes care of every concern Moses had. And despite his fears, Moses followed God's call—and led millions of Israelites to freedom.

If you want to be a part of God's great work in this world, perhaps the most helpful action step for you is to explore, identify, and overcome fears that keep you from pursuing God's calling in your life.

STEP 1. GIVE VOICE TO YOUR CALLING

If fears or other barriers didn't exist, what do you sense God might be calling you to do in this world? What "whisper" from him have you been ignoring? Write your thoughts in the space below.

STEP 2. IDENTIFY THE SOURCE OF YOUR FEAR

Below are some common types of fears that create barriers for leaders. Read the descriptions and explore your reactions.

Safety and Security—Fear about your personal safety (physically, mentally, emotionally, or spiritually); fear about financial or material stability for you or your family.

Ability and Confidence—Fear about having inadequate skills to accomplish the task; fear about managing the task with other responsibilities you have—family or otherwise.

Approval and Acceptance—Fear about whether others will approve and/or accept your calling; fear you may be rejected by people important to you.

Of the common fears listed, which one(s) most resonate as barriers that are holding you back from pursuing your calling?

What other fears are holding you back?

Describe how your past experiences or failures have contributed to your fear.

What is the worst thing that could happen if you wholeheartedly pursued your calling?

What is the best thing that could happen if you wholeheartedly pursued your calling?

STEP 3. GET GOD'S PERSPECTIVE

Sometimes, it is helpful to remind ourselves of God's truth when we are filled with fear. This exercise will help you identify God's voice. Just as God answered and encouraged Moses despite his fears, God will answer your fears with his sufficiency.

Read through the Scripture verses on the right, marking any that resonate strongly with you. How might really owning the truth of these verses help you face the fears you identified above? Write your thoughts in the "Reflections" column.

Reflections	Scripture Verses on Fear
	When I am afraid, I put my trust in you. (Psalm 56:3)
	Do not be anxious about anything, but in every situation, by prayer and petition, with thanksgiving, present your requests to God. And the peace of God, which transcends all understanding, will guard your hearts and your minds in Christ Jesus. (Philippians 4:6–7)
	Peace is what I leave with you; it is my own peace that I give you. I do not give it as the world does. Do not be worried and upset; do not be afraid. (John 14:27, GNT)
	Even though I walk through the valley of the shadow of death, I will fear no evil, for you are with me; your rod and your staff, they comfort me. (Psalm 23:4, ESV)
	Have I not commanded you? Be strong and courageous. Do not be afraid; do not be discouraged, for the LORD your God will be with you wherever you go. (Joshua 1:9)

Reflections	Scripture Verses on Fear

Therefore do not worry about tomorrow, for tomorrow will worry about itself. Each day has enough trouble of its own. (Matthew 6:34)

Do not worry about your life, what you will eat; or about your body, what you will wear. Life is more than food, and the body more than clothes. Consider the ravens: They do not sow or reap; they have no storeroom or barn; yet God feeds them. And how much more valuable you are than birds! Who of you by worrying can add a single hour to his life? Since you cannot do this very little thing, why do you worry about the rest? (Luke 12:22–26)

Cast your cares on the LORD and he will sustain you; he will never let the righteous be shaken. (Psalm 55:22)

For I am the LORD, your God, who takes hold of your right hand and says to you, "Do not fear; I will help you. Do not be afraid, for I myself will help you," declares the LORD, your Redeemer, the Holy One of Israel. (Isaiah 41:13–14)

God is our refuge and strength, an ever-present help in trouble. (Psalm 46:1)

Reflections	Scripture Verses on Fear
	I sought the LORD, and he answered me. He delivered me from all my fears. (Psalm 34:4)
	The LORD your God is in your midst, A victorious warrior. He will exult over you with joy, He will be quiet in His love, He will rejoice over you with shouts of joy. (Zephaniah 3:17, NASB)

If you think a particular verse or verses might help you face your area of fear, write the verse on a card and keep it in a prominent place (at your desk, on the bathroom mirror, etc.) to remind you of God's view in this area of your life.

STEP 4. PRAY ABOUT IT

Following God's calling doesn't guarantee us worldly success. But no matter the outcome, he promises to walk with us as we follow his lead. No matter where you are on your faith journey, there are likely places where fear makes it hard to follow what you sense is God's leading. Take a minute right now and ask him for clarity and courage in the area of your calling that gives you the greatest fear. Give your fear to him. If it would be helpful, write out your prayer below.

Today, God, I give you my fear of _____.

STEP 5. MAKE PLANS TO ADDRESS YOUR FEARS

Sometimes, taking simple steps to address your specific fears can help you move you forward toward your calling. Consider the ideas below as a starting point to help you. Highlight an idea that you think might help you. Or if none of them quite fit you, write in your own.

If your fear is safety or security related...

Make Plans:

Put safety nets in place to give you peace of mind.

- Meet with a financial planner and create a budget that will help you pursue your calling.

- Explore fund-raising opportunities that would help provide the financial resources necessary.

- Get more information about the security risks associated with your calling and if there are ways to mitigate them.

- If your calling includes reasonable fear for your physical safety:

  - Establish a will or put other legal documents in place to address your concerns.

  - Obtain life insurance.

- Other: _____

If your fear is ability or confidence related...	**Meet with Others:**
	o Set up coffee or lunch dates with people who know you well. Ask them to share with you what they see as your greatest strengths that might help you pursue this calling. Ask them to help you brainstorm solutions to barriers.
	o Meet with people who work in your area of calling to understand the skill set and experiences with which they entered their work.
	o Take a course or seminar to increase your skill level in areas needed.
	o Take a step of faith, and test your ability to figure it out and learn the skills needed as you go.
	o Other: _____
If your fear is approval or acceptance related...	**Bring Others Along—and Stand Firm:**
	o Include others in your exploration process through discussion, and introduce them through firsthand experiences that will help them understand your vision.
	o Explore the reasons behind a loved one's lack of approval, the validity of their point of view, and whether they would be willing to suspend judgment while you explore your calling.
	o Determine to stand firm in God's calling despite disapproval from others, knowing that he is faithful to stand alongside you—and that ultimately it is his approval you seek.
	o Other: _____

NOTE: If necessary, get professional help with your fears or anxiety

If your fear is significant and none of these steps seem doable to you, consider meeting with a licensed counselor who specializes in helping people overcome their fears and anxieties. He or she can help you understand your fear and work through it at a deeper level. Do not miss out on your calling due to fear! It is worth your time and money to understand your underlying issues—so you can get on to the business of living the life God calls you to live!

STEP 6. COMMIT TO YOUR NEXT STEP

In the next thirty days, commit to one action step that will begin to address your fears. Write your plan below and share it with a friend or mentor who can encourage your journey.

My Next Step Action is: _____

I will share this Action Step with: _____

I will accomplish this by: _____

This activity can take between one to two hours, depending on the depth of your reflection.

 Once you have completed your activity, go to Now What? on page 134 for additional ideas, next steps, and resources.

NOW WHAT?

You've now come full circle in your study. As you follow the direction in which God is leading you, it's time to step up and lead in it with all diligence. Now is the time to take responsibility for the next step of your leadership development and continue to apply what you have learned.

Bill stated that unless leaders are sure of their callings, it is difficult to make it to the end. It's simply too hard to lead in an area that doesn't ignite passion in your soul. When the dark days come, your clarity about your calling becomes the fuel you need to make it through. Seek God out in prayer for confirmation that you are where he wants you to be. Find encouragement and support in peers, mentors, and counselors. Be intentional about your spiritual and physical health by ensuring your spiritual and refreshment disciplines are in place. Your deepest connections to God—and your greatest learning and growth as a leader—will likely result from the hard days that come your way. Lean into God and be confident in his calling on your life.

As you continue on your leadership journey, remember to listen to God and stay leadable. He may call you to one mission for a season and then move you to something else. He is a magnificent orchestrator. He will encourage and sustain your leadership if you stay attuned to his whispers and purposes for your life.

My Action Plan – Pursue Your Unique Calling

Use the chart below to plan your next step(s) in Calling. Do you need to do some additional exploration to confirm the direction you think God wants you to go? Do you need additional self-assessment or training to gain the necessary skills? Or maybe you need to address fear or other issues that are holding you back. Write your next step(s) in the chart below—thinking through a realistic deadline and other people you will need to include in your plan.

Next Step	By When	Who should I include?	Who could help or coach me?

IT'S TIME
TO CELEBRATE

LEARNING GROUP GATHERING

CHECK-IN (15 minutes)

It's important to celebrate significant mile markers in your leadership journey. Schedule a final meeting with your learning group to share and commemorate the leadership skills you have acquired over the past months. You will not be watching a video or tackling new content, so make it a party to celebrate your leadership progress.

Debrief your Skills in Action activities around Calling. Use the following questions to guide your discussion.

- Which Skills in Action Activity did you complete?
- What did you learn about yourself and your calling?
- What next steps would be most helpful for you to continue to learn about and move into God's plan for your calling?

SUGGESTED TIME:
1 hour

Check-In:
15 minutes

Group Discussion:
40 minutes

Session Wrap-Up:
5 minutes

GROUP DISCUSSION (40 minutes)

1. Share the highlights for yourself and your team as you explored the different leadership topics covered in this study:

   - What were the most impactful messages for you and your team?

   - What were the most impactful activities for you and your team?

NEXT STEPS

2. Make plans for how you will continue your leadership growth, moving forward. Share your plans with your learning group.

List one or two activities that you would like to go back and do:

With yourself:

1) _____

2) _____

With your team:

1) _____

2) _____

3. Discuss future plans for your learning group. Might it be helpful to continue to meet to further encourage each other's leadership growth? What might that look like for your group and each individual?

The *Leading from Here to There* study has invited you on a journey to strengthen your skills in leadership. The teams and processes you lead will benefit from the investment you've made for years into the future. Way to go!

May God bless your leadership journey, and may you accomplish his purposes as you lead from *here* to *there*!

SESSION WRAP-UP (5 minutes)

Close your time in prayer together, thanking God for how he used this study in the lives of each person in the learning group and with their teams. Pray that each leader will take responsibility for their development, continue to grow, and lead with all diligence.

Join Bill Hybels at
The Global Leadership Summit

THE SUMMIT IS A TWO-DAY EVENT broadcast LIVE in HD from Willow's campus near Chicago every August to hundreds of locations in North America. Throughout the fall, Summit events take place in an additional 125+ countries.

More than an event, the Summit is a resource to be leveraged for community transformation. Leaders are discovering that by attending the Summit and utilizing its resources, their teams are increasing their impact. In fact, independent research shows that 83% of leaders who attended the Summit in consecutive years feel improved teamwork increased job satisfaction and productivity.

"Everyone wins when a leader gets better."
—Bill Hybels

INTERESTED IN HOSTING
THE GLOBAL LEADERSHIP SUMMIT
AT YOUR CHURCH OR ORGANIZATION?

GO TO WILLOWCREEK.COM/HOST

THE GLOBAL LEADERSHIP SUMMIT

Courageous Leadership

Field-Tested Strategy for the 360° Leader

Bill Hybels

Three-hundred-sixty-degree leaders don't just direct their gift of leadership south, to the people under their care. They also learn to lead north by influencing those with authority over them, and to lead east and west by impacting their peers. But most importantly, they learn how to keep the compass needle centered by leading themselves—by keeping their own lives in tune so they can provide maximum direction for others.

In what he considers his most important book, Bill Hybels shares what he has learned about Christian leadership in the thirty years he has pastored Willow Creek. *Courageous Leadership* offers proven leadership strategies already tested and refined in the trenches. Best of all, it gives you the very essence of one of today's foremost Christian leaders—his fervent commitment to evangelism and discipleship and his zeal to inspire fellow church leaders even as he seeks to keep growing as a leader himself.

"The local church is the hope of the world, and its future rests primarily in the hands of its leaders," Hybels insists.

If unchurched people matter to you ... if you love seeing believers serve passionately with their spiritual gifts ... if God's heartbeat for the church is your heartbeat as well ... then this book is a must. *Courageous Leadership* will convince you to lead with all your might, all your skill, and all your faith. And it will give you the tools to do just that.

Available in stores and online!